The
Allure
of the
Cat

The Allure of the Cat

Richard H. Gebhardt
John Bannon

Photos by Tetsu Yamazaki

T.F.H. Publications, Inc.

Distributed in the UNITED STATES by T.F.H. Publications, Inc., One T.F.H. Plaza, Neptune City, NJ 07753; in CANADA to the Pet Trade by H & L Pet Supplies Inc., 27 Kingston Crescent, Kitchener, Ontario N2B 2T6; Rolf C. Hagen Ltd., 3225 Sartelon Street, Montreal 382 Quebec; in CANADA to the Book Trade by Macmillan of Canada (A Division of Canada Publishing Corporation), 164 Commander Boulevard, Agincourt, Ontario M1S 3C7; in ENGLAND by T.F.H. Publications, PO Box 15, Waterlooville PO7 6BQ; in AUSTRALIA AND THE SOUTH PACIFIC by T.F.H. (Australia) Pty. Ltd., Box 149, Brookvale 2100 N.S.W., Australia; in NEW ZEALAND by Ross Haines & Son, Ltd., 82 D Elizabeth Knox Place, Panmure, Auckland, New Zealand; in the PHILIPPINES by Bio-Research, 5 Lippay Street, San Lorenzo Village, Makati, Rizal; in SOUTH AFRICA by Multipet Pty. Ltd., P.O. Box 35347, Northway, 4065, South Africa. Published by T.F.H. Publications, Inc. Manufactured in the United States of America by T.F.H. Publications, Inc.

INTRODUCTION

Cats have fascinated people for thousands of years. This fascination starts at an early age. Eight year old Bernie Degen draws cats "because I love them and they love me. They are my friend when I need a friend...otherwise they leave me alone."

Maybe this eight year old boy summed it all up. People who love cats love them passionately. People who dislike cats never really knew one.

This book is the culmination of the love for cats. The Japanese photographer Tetsu Yamazaki has dedicated his life to cat photography. He constantly travels the world to photograph cat shows and to see the newer varieties. His photos were used to represent the most beautiful cats in his huge file of cat photographs. Mr. Yamazaki selected these photos just for this book. They are truly representatives of the various breeds.

CONTENTS

48	48	48	48	55	55
ABYSSINIAN, RUDDY	ABYSSINIAN, SORREL	ABYSSINIAN, FAWN	ABYSSINIAN, BLUE	AMERICAN CURL, BLUE	AMERICAN CURL, BLACK & WHITE

CONTENTS

Norwegian Forest Cat, blue mackerel tabby. This 10 month old male novice still has the appearance of the wild cat.

The Family of Cats

The domestic cat is one of about 38 wild felids that are found on most continents of the world, other than Australia and Antarctica. They are most numerous in the warmer areas of our planet but some, such as the Siberian tiger, will range into the arctic circle. Zoologists place cats in the family Felidae, which is one of many sorts of pigeonholes, called ranks, within the system of scientific classification. The idea of formal classification, also known as *taxonomy* or *systematics*, is to arrange all lifeforms into a logical order that attempts to show the believed phylogenetic (evolutionary) relationships of all the animals on our planet.

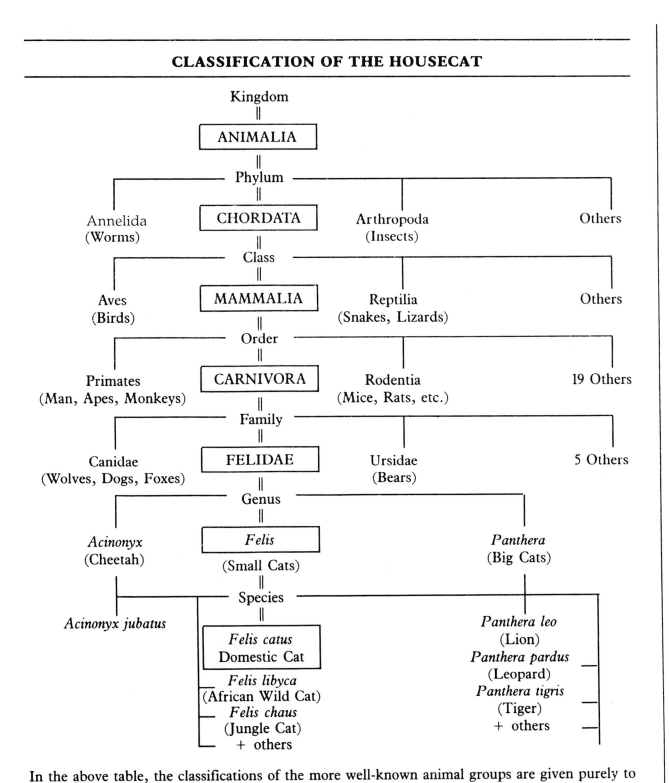

CLASSIFICATION OF THE HOUSECAT

Kingdom
‖
ANIMALIA
‖
Phylum
‖
Annelida (Worms) — **CHORDATA** — Arthropoda (Insects) — Others
‖
Class
‖
Aves (Birds) — **MAMMALIA** — Reptilia (Snakes, Lizards) — Others
‖
Order
‖
Primates (Man, Apes, Monkeys) — **CARNIVORA** — Rodentia (Mice, Rats, etc.) — 19 Others
‖
Family
‖
Canidae (Wolves, Dogs, Foxes) — **FELIDAE** — Ursidae (Bears) — 5 Others
‖
Genus
‖
Acinonyx (Cheetah) — *Felis* (Small Cats) — *Panthera* (Big Cats)
‖
Species
‖
Acinonyx jubatus

Felis catus Domestic Cat
Felis libyca (African Wild Cat)
Felis chaus (Jungle Cat)
+ others

Panthera leo (Lion)
Panthera pardus (Leopard)
Panthera tigris (Tiger)
+ others

In the above table, the classifications of the more well-known animal groups are given purely to show the believed degree of their relationships with cats.

The basis of the system is that it commences with the kingdom called *Animalia*. In this is found every animal (as compared to plant) on our planet. This means that the animal kingdom embraces every organism from the microscopic to the blue whale, which is the largest animal on earth. The kingdom is divided into many groups called *phyla* (singular: *phylum*). Each of these contains all those animals which share certain features. Each phylum is divided into many classes on the same basis. These in turn are divided into orders, and the orders into families and so on.

Within each rank, or taxon, the members are a mutually inclusive group all having many of the same collective features. The lower the rank in the system the more the animals begin to resemble one another. The lowest obligate rank in the system is that of the species. At this level all the members are quite clearly very closely related — yet differences can still be observed. So regional varieties are known as subspecies.

A species is a group of individuals that will freely interbreed in their wild habitat. They will produce fertile offspring that display all of the combined features of their parents. They may of course show very minor differences in their color, or coat pattern, and will differ somewhat in size, yet clearly resemble their parents. Such differences that they may display are the features that make them individuals. There may be very obvious differences between the male and the female of a given species. As long as the individuals of a given sex resemble their parent of that sex, they are still an example of that species.

CLASSIFICATION OF THE CATS

In order that you can understand animal classification we can look at the way cats are accommodated in this classification. Rather than start at the species level, it is more convenient to begin rather higher in the system. We will commence with the rank known as a *class*. There are several classes of vertebrate (backboned) animals. You will at once notice certain differences between the following animals: a bird, a snake, a fish, and a cat. Each of them is a member of a distinctive class of animals:

Aves — birds. Possess feathers and scales, have no teeth and lay eggs.

Reptilia — the snakes, lizards, crocodiles, turtles, etc. Possess scales, may have no limbs. Many other features that make them reptiles.

Osteichthyes — the bony fish. Their skeleton made entirely of bone. Most have scales, breathe through gills.

Mammalia — the mammals. Have hair, suckle their young.

Although only obvious features are indicated, there are in fact many other features that would place an animal into one of these groups. The system works on the basis of considering all characteristics, then placing the animal into the most appropriate 'pigeonhole'. If an animal carries a number of features seen in others, it is reasonable to suppose that those features were derived from a common ancestor at some point in time. As a result, it can be seen that the further up the system you go the further back in time it will be when examples from a given rank would have shared a common origin. This will be explained better at the end of the discussion.

The class Mammalia is divided into a number of groups called orders. A few of these are cited which contain many animals you will be familiar with.

Rodentia — the mice, rats, guinea pigs and their like.

Lagomorpha — rabbits and hares.

Primates — monkeys, apes and humans.

Cetacea — whales, dolphins and porpoises.

Artiodactyla — pigs, sheep, hippos, giraffes, deer, camels.

Carnivora — dogs, cats, bears, hyenas, skunks, seals, raccoons, otters and others.

In each of these orders the members are characterized by a number of features. They all have things in common with those from other orders — they all suckle their young and they all have hair — even the whales, which are air breathing just the same as we are. The features of Carnivora are that they are all adapted to live, to a greater or lesser degree, on the flesh of other animals. They have teeth developed with this end in mind, and a digestive system that is relatively short when compared to non-carnivores.

The carnivores are divided into a number of families. Three examples of these are the bears (Ursidae), the wolves, foxes and dogs (Canidae) and the cats (Felidae). At this level in the system of classification the affinities between the members are very apparent. The cats, in spite of the great difference in sizes displayed, are quite clearly cats, as compared to bears or dogs, which are equally distinctive. There are always a few oddballs that might be difficult to recognize. Generally you would have no problems recognizing members of the cat, dog or bear families. Cats have very distinctive coat patterns and colors. They usually have claws which can be withdrawn into sheaths when not in use. They have very well developed canine or dagger teeth. Their bodies are extremely supple, and most species have long tails (the lynx and bobcat being notable exceptions). The muzzle is foreshortened when compared to other carnivores, which allows for a greater mouth arc when the cats are about to bite their victim. The characteristic number of genes for the family is 38 (19 pairs) in most species.

Families are divided into *genera* (singular: *genus*). There are just three of these usually recognized in the family Felidae (though some scientists accept several others). Two are quite clearly similar, but the third contains an example that is so different from the others it is termed monogeneric, meaning it contains but a single species. This genus is *Acinonyx*. It accommodates the cheetah, the fastest mammal on our planet. Its claws are non-retractable. It has special 'treads' on its paws to help in turning and braking at high speed. It has always given taxonomists a problem. Most of its features are quite clearly feline, so it is simply regarded as an aberrant form. (Fossils show that cheetahs evolved from an ancestor related to the American cougar.)

John R. Quinn '90

The Puma, Cougar or Mountain Lion, whatever you choose to call him, is scientifically known as *Felis concolor*.

The other two genera are *Panthera* and *Felis*. The former contains the big or roaring cats — lions, tigers, jaguars and leopards. *Felis* houses all other cats, normally termed the small cats. The differences between the two genera are linked to the fact that the big cats can roar, but can purr only when they exhale. Small cats can purr continuously. The puma, cougar, or mountain lion, *Felis concolor*, is the largest of the small cats, while the leopard is the smallest of the big cats.

Cheetah, *Acinonyx jubatus.*

John R. Quinn '90

Pallas' Cat, *Felis manul.*

Kodkod, *Felis guigna.*

Geoffroy's Cat, Felis geoffroyi.

Clouded Leopard, *Panthera nebulosa.*

Martelli's Wild Cat, *Felis lumensis,* is now considered extinct.

The genus is divided into a number of species that are characterized by their size, bodily form, color and patterns. The lion and tiger are clearly very similar in many respects, yet are equally obviously not of the same 'sort' of cat. In the same way, the ocelot and the serval are obviously small cats, but are quite easily distinguished each from the other.

It is clear from the system that if you could go back in time you would come to the common ancestor of the serval and the ocelot before you would arrive at the common ancestor between either of these and that of a lion. Likewise, the common ancestor of any cat would be met before you came to the common ancestor of a cat and a dog. Your cat and yourself share more in common than a goldfish or canary would have with either of you. The system is thus termed a natural system of classification, because it is thought that the relationships of members at any rank are believed to be real. Of course, this may not actually be so. Especially at the lower ranks, experts will argue with each other on the relative importance that is attached to given features when deciding into which pigeonhole an animal should be placed. Cats have always been at the center of such debates. A cat regarded as a species by one person is viewed as being a subspecies by another. They have been moved across genera, and genera themselves have been abandoned and reinstated over the years. Presently, most experts agree to place all small cats in the single genus of *Felis.* This is more a convenience than a true reflection of the likely phylogeny of the species but is where we are at presently.

SCIENTIFIC NAMES

All scientific animal names are based on the use of the Latin language. The system is accepted by every country in the world. An animal can have any number of common names, because these are not controlled, other than by popular usage. Scientific names are controlled by international codes, which are supervised by appointed bodies of experts. The rank of genus and species is always indicated in a typeface that differs from the main body of text in which it appears. This invariably means that it usually is printed in italics or underlined. The generic name always begins with a capital letter, while the specific or trivial name always commences with a lowercase letter. A species can only be identified when both the genus and the specific name are stated together. For example, *Felis concolor* is the mountain lion. Any number of animals can have the specific name of *concolor*, but when this is paired to *Felis* it is unique to just that species. It is thus a binomial, and the system is called the binomial system of nomenclature.

Species often are very variable. If the variations (in size, colors, proportions, etc.) are restricted geographically, subspecies may be recognized. To accommodate this situation a trinomial is created. The original (nominate) form has its specific name repeated, while each of the other forms has its own trinomial added to the species name. Thus: *Felis concolor concolor*, the eastern cougar; *Felis coryi*, the Florida cougar. There are many more aspects to formal classification, but those detailed cover the main essentials of the system in its use.

THE ANCESTOR OF THE DOMESTIC CAT

The domestic cat is given the scientific name of *Felis catus*, formerly *Felis domesticus*, by some scientists. It is given species status largely because no one is sure from which species it came. There are three running favorites:

Felis silvestris — European Wild Cat (7 subspecies)

Felis libyca — African Wild Cat (19 subspecies)

Felis chaus — Jungle Cat (9 subspecies)

I doubt very much that it will ever be determined from which the domestic cat came, though most experts favor *libyca*. (Actually, many mammalogists today call the domestic cat *Felis silvestris*, with *F. libyca* and *F. catus* synonyms.) The problem is that both *libyca* (especially) and *chaus* skulls have been found in Egyptian burial grounds. Both enjoy distribution in the general area (northern Africa-Middle East) where it is assumed domestication commenced. Both will hybridize with each other, and with *catus* and *sylvestris*. Clearly, all of these are extremely closely related genetically. The body structure of each of the wild species is

Black-footed Cat, *Felis nigripes*.

Spanish Lynx, *Felis pardina*.

Flat-headed Cat, *Felis planiceps*.

Rusty-spotted Cat, *Felis rubiginosa*.

African Golden Cat, *Felis aurata*.

very similar — to the degree that one could not say for certain that the domestic cat was of this or that species.

There is no doubt that *sylvestris* is the more ferocious of the trio. This is not sufficient reason to rule it out, as at least one very gentle offspring has been recorded from crosses with domestic cats. It is quite possible that all three may have had a hand in the domestication process. Some authorities believe that *libyca*

European Wildcat, *Felis sylvestris.*

and *chaus* are no more than subspecies of *sylvestris*, so one could say it's really not even a matter of academic importance.

How Was the Cat Domesticated?

There are two ways any animal can be domesticated. One is by examples being captured and then bred from. The other is by what I would term a familiarity process. It is most likely that it was by the familiarity process, which is both easier and more reliable. The way it would have happened is very simple. As the early humans settled into permanent abodes they grew cereal crops, and produced garbage. This attracted rodents, and these attracted local wild cats.

These cats thus found a relatively easy means of feeding themselves on unusually large numbers of one of their regular prey species. Those which had a greater disposition not to fear humans would eventually settle down and breed in the immediate vicinity of the settlements. It only becomes a matter of time before a human is able to acquire one of the kittens as a house pet. This, assuming a female, would soon produce a litter of kittens. Some of these would be passed to others in the settlement. Over any span of time the less 'domestic' of the kittens would wander off to be feral, or totally wild. Those that remained would represent the cats with a greater genetic makeup in the 'placid' end of the potential temperament spectrum. Domestication can thus appear (and disappear) in many places at the same time, depending on the terrain, the species of animal concerned, and the overall conditions that exist, and which would make domestication a possibility. If you would like to read more about the relatives of the domestic cat and their evolution, you are advised to obtain the *Atlas of Cats of the World* by Dennis Kelsey-Wood, published by T.F.H. Publications, Inc. of New Jersey.

Domestic Cat History

It is not known exactly when the cat set foot on the path to domestication, because this may well have happened before recorded history began. This fact has never been established with any degree of certainty. In tracing the history of any long established domestic animal, it is often a case of piecing together bits of information and drawing conclusions from them. At the same time, given our present knowledge of the wild cat species, and of our own history, it is possible to theorize on the conditions that would be needed to bring a cat into a domestic state. A calculated guess at when this happened, and where, can then be made.

CONDITIONS FOR FELINE DOMESTICATION

Before any animal or plant was domesticated there must first have been a need for this process to take place. The earliest humans were nomadic hunter-gatherers. Some eventually settled near watercourses and lived essentially on the fish and other animals of the seas or rivers. Others moved constantly, following the migration routes of the mammals they hunted. Not until they settled to form larger communities, which exhibited a high degree of differentiation of labor, thus organization, could civilization begin. As the hunter-gatherers moved towards the beginnings of semi-permanent settlements, so they began to domesticate certain animals that were easily controlled. The auroch (a wild cow), sheep, pigs and gamebirds were the first domesticated species — along with the dog, which was probably the first animal to strike up an association with humans. Each of these animals offered very obvious benefits to humans, mostly as a source of food and clothing — the dog being the exception in that it was essentially a hunting companion and guard. Although humans flirted with agriculture about 12,500BC, it apparently didn't last. By 10,000BC it seems they had returned to the hunter-gatherer style of living. It is thought that changing climatic conditions brought about the failure of our first experiments to be farmers. Not for another 4-5 millennia would crop growing become a major feature of humans.

Until at least this time there was no need for humans to keep cats, nor for cats to dwell with them. The benefit of the cat could only be felt when human settlements had reached that point where rats, mice, and other rodents were becoming a pest by their growing numbers. While humans were nomadic, these creatures were no real problem. Further, cats, unlike dogs, are not disposed to range over too large a territory, especially the smaller felines. The cat was not dependent on larger game in order to survive, its needs being found locally to its habitat. Humans and dogs lived a comparable life and had a comparable social structure. Their early association was almost inevitable.

The need of humans for cats was essentially a triad of conditions, each bound up in the other. Firstly, it needed humans to reach a high degree of proficiency in agriculture, especially crop growing. Secondly, arising out of the first condition, would be the need for humans to live a settled life, which implies larger communities and fixed dwellings. Finally, these two conditions would create the ideal environment for rodents to move in by their millions. These fed on the crops, as well as on the growing amounts of garbage, which are a feature of all human habitation. Even the corpses of humans represented an increasing storehouse of food for this highly successful group of mammals. Their very way of life meant that, apart from the considerable cost to farmers in lost grain, there was the obvious risk of spreading disease.

THE FIRST CIVILIZATIONS

Given that the conditions under which a cat would be most welcome have been outlined, it then becomes a case of applying dates and locations for when and where the process of domestication may have commenced. It happens that civilization began in the fertile crescent created by the Tigris and Euphrates rivers, as well as in the fertile lands to the west of these, which were formed by the river Nile. The beginnings of civilization are apparent by about 5,000BC. By the end of the next millennium large towns were appearing. The standard of living had progressed considerably.

However, if Egypt is taken as an example, the excavations at places such as Badari, Naquada, Abu Simbel, and Maadi all strongly suggest that the cat had not appeared on the scene by 3,000BC. The reason for stating this is based on the findings in necropolis sites at the places named, along with very many others. In the tombs of the kings, as well as in the graves of lesser mortals, there was much found that indicated the way of life. Furniture, food, pots, amulets, tools, and statuettes depict life in those days. There are carvings of the lion, falcon, ibis, bull, fish, donkey, hippo, snakes and other reptiles, and, of course, the ubiquitous dog. But there are none of cats, which surely would have been included if they were a familiar, or even an exotic, inhabitant of Egyptian homes at this period.

It would seem that it was not until the Middle Kingdom in Egypt (2040-1640BC) that the cat begins to appear. During this period the mummified remains of cats were found at Beni Hasan and other sites. These were shipped to England and sold as fertilizer — a total of nineteen tons of them from diggings created when the Suez canal was being built. This represented an estimated 80,000 cats. Clearly, by this period cats had become extremely popular, as had baboons — judging by the packed mummified remains of these primates still to be seen in the necropolis at Tuna el Gebel.

Although it is generally held that the cat was first domesticated in Egypt the fact that it does not appear until the Middle Kingdom might suggest that it was imported from lands to the north and east. The obvious areas would have been Palestine, Syria or even Turkey (then the land of the Hittites). It is from these areas that Egypt obtained the domesticated ass, horse and other livestock, as well as the chariot. Egypt had traded with these countries for well over a thousand years by the Middle Kingdom times. Little information can be found in cat books in relation to the early domestication of felids. There is certainly a need for data to be collected from other sources.

THE CAT CULT

The reason Egypt is of such interest to feliophiles is that it was to give rise to the cult of the cat, Bast or Bastet. I will give a little more detail than is usually seen in cat books because I am sure many cat owners will find this a most interesting topic. From their very beginnings Egyptian chiefs, and the dynasties of pharaohs they were to become, worshiped their gods in the form of animal-headed humans. Examples are *Horus*, the falcon, *Anubis*, the dog, and *Apis*, the bull. Pakhet, the lioness goddess, is one of many deities that featured the king of the beasts. The cat was rather late on the scene in this respect but was to progress from a city deity to that of national status in the pantheon of Egypt.

Bast was named for Bubastis, which is located in the Nile Delta. It was a city of ancient origin, but became especially important when the Libyan kings of the Twenty Second dynasty (1070-712BC) made it their main base of residence. This gave further impetus to the already successful cult. Bast was originally a lioness-goddess but became a domestic cat at a date not established. The goddess represented gentle passion, especially sex and maternal love. She also protected men from disease and evil spirits. At the annual feasts that celebrated the deities, that of Bast was especially popular. The fact that it involved much wine drinking, merriment, and probably orgies, ensured it was a winner from the outset! People traveled vast distances to attend the feast. Bast is said to have been related to the god Amon, and was the wife of Ptah, a very powerful god of Memphis who became one of Egypt's most respected deities.

It was the custom to bury the mummified remains of cats within the shadows of the Bast temples, and many people would take their beloved cats there in order to do just this. This is the origin of the vast cemeteries of mummified cats found at various locations in Egypt. At Beni Hasam, Bast was worshiped in her secondary form of Pakhet, the lioness goddess already mentioned. At some of the Bast ceremonies even the pharaoh would officiate.

Bast's form was of a cat-headed women who held a semicircular breastplate surmounted

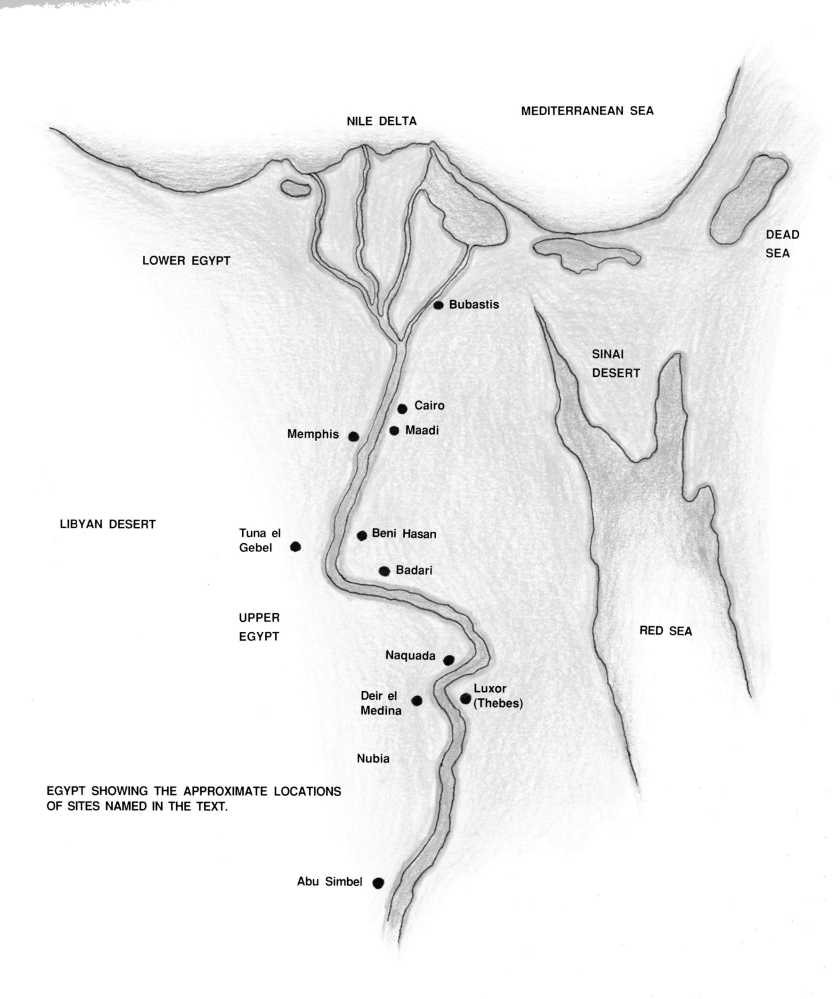

EGYPT SHOWING THE APPROXIMATE LOCATIONS
OF SITES NAMED IN THE TEXT.

with a lioness's head in her right hand, and a small basket in her left hand, both hands being held together at mid body line. Although the cult of Bast was evident in the early New Kingdom (1550-1070BC) it gained a tremendous boost after the reign of Amenhotop 1V (Akhenaten), the 10th pharaoh of the 18th dynasty. This pharaoh banned all deities other than his chosen favorite Aten (the sun god). In particular, he destroyed as many references as he could to Amon (the ram-headed god) and those related to Amon's trinity. This included Bast. Following the pharaoh's death, his son, the famous young king Tutankhaten (living image of Aten) changed his own name to Tutankhamon, or Tutankhamun, (living image of Amon) and reintroduced all of the former gods. From this time onward, the animal deities would gain in support, in line with the steady decline in the image of the pharaohs as the incarnation of god on earth. This reached a peak in the period of the Libyan pharaohs (946-712BC). Not until these gods were banned by the Romans in AD390 did cat worship decline, at least officially — but old beliefs die hard.

THE POWER OF THE CAT CULT

Unlike many other animal cults, which were often local or regional, the cat cult was practiced throughout the Egyptian world. These people, as the Greeks and later the Romans were to observe, took their beliefs extremely seriously. It is worth quoting the comments of Diodorus Siculus, a Greek historian, on the matter of sacred animals: ' when one of these animals is concerned, he who kills one, be it accidentally or maliciously, is put to death'. He continues 'superstition towards these sacred animals is deeply rooted in the Egyptian's soul, and devotion to their cult is passionate'. He goes on to tell of a Roman who accidentally killed a cat. 'The populace crowded to the house of the Roman and neither the efforts of magistrates sent by the king to protect him, nor the universal fear inspired by the might of Rome, could avail to save the man's life.'

Another Greek historian, Herodotus, also witnessed the power of the cat cult when he noted that if a house caught fire the cat was the first thing to be rescued, its value, and the pain of its loss, being greater than any other possession.

DAY-TO-DAY LIFE OF A CAT

We can gain some glimpse of the everyday life of Egyptian cats through the many fine paintings that have survived the centuries. For example, on the walls of a workman's tomb in Deir el Medina, circa 1,400BC, can be seen a cat stealing fish from a funerary offering. On another wallpainting dating from about the same period, and found in Thebes (now Luxor), a tabby cat is seen grasping the wings of a bird in flight. The bird is on a small skiff, together with its owner and his family, in a portrayal of an idealized life of hunting in the marshes.

Apart from the wall and tomb paintings, evidence of the cat's high status is also seen in the bronze and wooden coffins in which the 'better off' cats were laid to rest. Some of these even had mummified mice with them so they would not go hungry in the next life! Progressively, from the New Kingdom onwards, the followers of Bast made many small statues of seated cats which would be kept in their homes. Some of these would have nose rings or earrings of gold. It is quite possible that their cats may actually have worn earrings because we do know that sacred crocodiles were fitted with golden bracelets on their legs.

The people of Egypt were not allowed to enter the cult temples, and the only time they would see their god was at the yearly festivals when the god or goddess statues were taken from their sites and carried on boats around the outer walls of the temple. At all other times they would worship their chosen god(s) in their homes and could contact the real thing via temple priests.

THE SPREAD OF THE CAT

Making due allowance for the fact that the cat may not have been domesticated in Egypt, it is generally held that it was from this country that it spread to the rest of the world. This may, however, be true — at least for certain cats. Let us presuppose that the cat was already domesticated when it was taken to Egypt from elsewhere. In its new homeland it becomes venerated to a far higher level than in its former home.

It must be assumed that the Egyptians, especially the temple priests, became proficient breeders. This so, there is no doubt, over the spans of time involved, that pure strains, or even varieties, would be developed. It is these, rather than the everyday cat of the lands, that may have had great value, especially if they came from temple stock. If this situation happened, then one can readily appreciate that their export was banned by the Egyptians. Such cats would command very high values — as compared to your regular street or country cat. It must be remembered that the history of cats passed down to us, such that it is, was written by those such as Herodotus, who was as much a storyteller as a historian. He may not, as good a historian as he was, have made the distinction between well-bred felids and mongrels (moggies). Further, it is thought that much of his information was secondhand. It may have been altered in the telling.

It may therefore be that quality cats were exported from Egypt to the immediate lands around them. The first European countries they would be taken to would have been the island states of Crete and Cyprus, and from there to mainland Greece and Italy. As far as the eastern spread of the cat goes, this may well have taken place during the Assyrian, Persian and Hellenistic periods of Egypt, which commenced during the Late Period (712-332BC).

Neither the Greeks nor the Romans held the cat in quite the same esteem as had the Egyptians. The immediate Eastern countries had even less regard for them. Nonetheless, the Romans in particular did think highly of their cats, even if this fell short of actual worship. They took them wherever their armies traveled. In this way the cat spread to Spain, through France, and then into Britain, Germany and Holland.

References as to when the cat was actually introduced to Britain seem rather unreliable to this author. The date often cited is circa AD900. This would not seem in keeping with the fact that the Romans invaded Britain before the birth of Christ, and that by the date given, the Roman Empire had collapsed some five centu-

ries earlier. Be this as it may, once established, the cat did well in Britain for a few centuries.

CHANGING FORTUNES OF THE CAT

The cat's love affair with humans in Western Europe largely came to an end as a result of the purges of the church — which had been the basis behind it being a banned cult back in Egypt a few hundred years earlier. The relationship of the cat with pagan cults was the obvious cause of the cat's downfall. It was persecuted in the most horrendous manner in the period from about the 13th to the 17th centuries. During this period there was considerable persecution of any form of heresy. It seems that the cat was associated with both the Bogomils, and later with the Cathars, both heretical Christian beliefs. With its added association with witches throughout this period, the poor cat came to be blamed for every problem that happened.

However, in spite of these setbacks the cat survived and was even tolerated as long as it stayed out of people's houses. Its benefit on farms, and in helping keep the rampant rodent population at bay, could not even be overlooked by the church. By the end of the 17th century the cat was coming back into favor with all and had even begun to win over members of the clergy. As the 18th and 19th centuries unfurled, the cat became more and more popular. By the end of the latter century a new 'cult of the cat' was in evidence — the arrival of cat shows and the development of the breeds.

THE CAT IN THE EAST

While in Europe the cat was going through bad times, things were rather better as one moved East. This was because the entire religious and political scenes were different. Christianity was not the major force it was in the West, and the further East one went the more we see animals remaining a vital part of religion and mythology, a situation that pertains to this day. The cat was not a major part of the pantheons of the many countries in Asia and the Far East, but it was regarded in most as a creature that could ward off evil spirits. As such it was given reasonable treatment, being highly valued by some, depending on their particular leanings.

The ills of the people in various countries could be blamed on other things, usually demons and the malevolent humanlike gods. The thinking of these Asiatic and Far Eastern peoples was totally different from the monotheist thoughts of Western ideology. The status of the cat was thus much as it is to this day, being a spectrum that ranges from total indifference to that of a favored pet. On the down side it has to be said that it was, and remains, a food item to some peoples, such as those in parts of Korea. However, the monkey and the dog are also included in the same food list, so it is not a case that the cat alone is singled out. In condemning such practices it should not be forgotten that Western people to this very day take delight in owning coats and other items made from the skins of wild cat species.

Cats have evolved color-wise and hair-wise, but their basic hunting instincts have remained intact. Cats enjoy catching toy mice dangled on the end of a stick.

THE CAT IN AMERICA AND AUSTRALIA

When the Pilgrim fathers left England, along with all of the other peoples of Europe who were being persecuted for their beliefs, they took their cats with them. In this way the cat entered the colonies of the Americas during the 17th century, possibly even a little earlier. The persecutions that the Pilgrims had sought to evade in England were, however, to reappear in the colonies. As a result the cat was again involved, but for a lesser time and to a much lesser degree. There was a new nation to be opened up. This called for the shedding of worn-out doctrines.

As families moved ever westward the cat moved as well. Kittens became quite valuable because of the need to protect grain stores from the ravages of rodents, of which there were more species in America than in England. The clock of time had turned full circle. The practical benefits that had made the cat so valuable in ancient Egypt were again sought after. The situation was much the same in Australia, where the feline population rises annually, as it does in every country in the world where there is a need to control rodents, and where the beauty of the cat is appreciated.

IN CONCLUSION

From the foregoing text you will see that the domestic cat has been both worshiped and hated during the course of its long history. It is perhaps a little surprising that its domestication can only be verified for a period rather shorter than many people may have thought. However, as more research is done it is quite probable that the history of the cat will be pushed backwards in time. There are still many gaps to be filled, and many questions remain unanswered. There is certainly a need for all the data that is known to be gathered together and published in a single volume. Maybe such a work will one day be forthcoming. The history of the individual breeds is dealt with under the appropriate breed names.

Aspects of Cat Breeds

Although the cat as a domestic species may have been around for a couple of thousand or so years, the breeds you can see at shows, and in books, are all relatively recent creations. Indeed, very few can claim a pure lineage for more than about one hundred years. Of course, as is quite common in many animal hobbies, you will hear breeders boasting that their particular breed can be traced back hundreds of years. Within the cat fancy there are those who really believe their cats are directly linked to the cats of the pharaohs. There is no harm done in such thinking, as it adds spice to conversations. Every cat alive today could actually claim direct lineage to the pharaonic cats, because this was probably their line of descent during domestication. We must therefore establish some sort of guidelines to determine what we are calling breeds. There are really two forms, one being much older than the other, and more questionable in terms of its genetic pureness.

BREED DEFINITION

Type Breeds: These are the breeds that have been known to exist for many years. They are often referred to as being natural, though no domestic cat can claim such status — only good species can be natural. However, in the context of domestic cats, they are breeds such as the Persian, the Angora, the Siamese, or any of the 'street' breeds. The street breeds embrace those cats that are local to a country, or region, and which have retained the same appearance over many years. In actual fact, street cats are hardly breeds because they represent the average gene pool of a given region. As such they are really mongrels, or moggies as they are referred to in the world of the cat fancy. Clearly, Persians have a more obvious type than your regular shorthaired cat about town. This does not mean that every Persian looking cat is necessarily pure of lineage.

The ancestors of a given Persian-looking cat could have been shorthaired, Siamese, curly coated or any other type. The pointed Persians of today's show cats can all be traced back to Siamese crosses with Persians. It can be seen that some breeds can lay greater claim to such status than can others. Indeed, some cats within a breed are more pure than are others.

Pure Breeds: The essential difference between a type breed and a pure breed is that the pure breed's purity of genotype can be proven. The only way this is possible is by documentation in the form of pedigrees, and by a written standard that clearly states what a given breed looks like. Such a standard cannot be vague. It must detail the features of a breed to the degree that it could not be confused with any other. The members of that breed must be capable of passing on all of the essential features that will ensure their offspring are basically an image of themselves. The pedigree of the cat in question must have been lodged with an accredited association, and the cat registered with that association from birth. In this way its lineage can be proven as far as is possible.

Given the data needed to fulfill the definition of a pure breed, it will be readily appreciated that the oldest pure breeds can go no further back in time than that point when stud books were established for the breed in question. This, in effect, means no pure breed can predate the beginnings of the formation of the oldest cat clubs, which commenced in England just before and just after the turn of the 20th century. Now, it is true that pedigrees predate the formation of cat clubs, but anyone can write out their own pedigree, which has no value if it is in isolation of a stud book and a written standard.

It can be seen that of the oldest breeds seen today they must, of necessity, have developed from type breeds. If you have a Persian or Siamese cat it may be possible to trace its ancestors to the first of the breed that were registered. However, beyond that nothing can be proven. One or more generations before that, it may have included the genes of some other 'breed,' so its pureness of descent is immediately terminated. It becomes a cat of mixed ancestry, even if that ancestry was predominately of a Persian or another given type. This applies to every breed of cat seen today.

Breeds by Association of Features

Sometimes people will link the likeness of a present day cat to a painting or carving done hundreds of years ago, and use this to support the view that a given breed is extremely old. Such conclusions could, of course, be correct. The chances are remote in the extreme. For one thing, paintings done centuries ago are rarely detailed enough to establish anything other than the fact that certain types existed. Spotted cats have been known since the earliest days of feline domestication, as have tabbies, and cats of the Siamese or foreign type. Longhaired cats have been in existence for many centuries. This does not mean they are Persians, no more than a foreign type seen in a painting is a Korat or an Egyptian Mau.

Even if a present day cat has an especially significant feature, such as no tail, or no hair, it would be misleading to suppose that it was related to a similar cat seen on a painting five centuries earlier. Such features are brought about by mutation. These are spontaneous happenings that can occur in differing locations at differing times. They can happen in any breed. They can alter the entire visual appearance of a cat. The rex mutation, which happened in normal shorthaired British cats, resulted in the kittens looking like cats of a foreign breed.

Type breeds may have been created in past ages, but a breed is not necessarily a continuum, so while a breed of today could resemble a breed of past times, the two may have no direct relationship. The earlier breed may have died out years ago. A look-alike statue or painting may simply have been one cat that happened to resemble a present-day breed.

An Egyptian Mau poses with an Egyptian statuette. Photo by Robert Pearcy.

Breed Creation

The foregoing text is applicable to those breeds that have retained an obvious type over many years. Most breeds you can select from are much younger, and have only been around for fifty years or less. They are the result of either mutations that have appeared, or have been created by crossings involving established breeds, or crossing established breeds with mutational breeds. A number of breeds are at this time still being developed. They will not gain official status until they have firmly established their type, and are supported by a good nucleus of breeders. Normally, it requires at least five generations before the major registration bodies will accept them. It is for this reason we have pedigreed cats and not purebred cats. Most associations have not taken a stand on how many generations, if any, determine a breed to be purebred or a pure breed.

The Basis of a Breed

Cats do not exhibit anything like the variation in size and general conformation that is seen in dogs, rabbits or horses. This so, breed status is based on color, hair type, hair length, and any feature that is the result of a mutation affecting the bodily parts — such as ear shape, the lack of hair, the lack of a tail, or its foreshortening. Some breeds are very distinctive, while others look very similar, the color alone being sufficient to give breed status. This makes things a little more confusing to the first-time purebred cat owner. There is a reason for this situation, though it does seem at times.

For example, if a breed was originally recognized in certain colors, and then new ones appear, this can create controversy. The estab-

lished breeders may take the view that the color was introduced from another breed. This constitutes cross-breeding and may not be acceptable to those in the breed. Those with the new colors have no alternative but to give their cats a new name, even though in all other respects the 'new breed' is the same as the old one except for its color. The basis of the controversy is clearly whether or not the color was a natural mutation within the original breed, or whether it was in fact introduced by hybridization. Any changes in appearance this creates can be bred out over the next few generations by breeding back to the original breed.

The same arguments tend to arise when specimens of an established breed suddenly appear with long hair. The obvious question is 'was the long hair introduced or did it appear as a natural mutation? ' It is usual in many animal hobbies to give the longhaired variants their own breed status. Some breed societies are more tolerant than others where color is concerned. Unless the color(s) is the basis of a breed, most of the newer breeds will not be restricted over this.

BREED RECOGNITION

Not all cat breeds have equal recognition with the varying cat registration bodies. The older, well established, breeds will be recognized by all governing bodies, but newer breeds may not be. Further, some breeds accepted by one or two associations may never be acceptable as breeds to others. For example, the Governing Council of the Cat Fancy (GCCF) in Great Britain will never recognize breeds that are derived from mutations that are known to be associated with genetic defects likely to be deleterious in any way. The exception to this is the Manx, which is one of the oldest of all cat breeds.

In the USA the Cat Fanciers' Association (CFA) also applies very stringent regulations along much the same lines. Other associations may be more liberal.

BREED NAMES AND COLORS

Although most breed names are the same regardless of which side of the Atlantic you live on, a few do change as you cross the water. For example, the Persian of the USA is known simply as the Longhair in Great Britain. In the USA the colors of the Persian are merely varieties of the breed. In the UK the colors within the Longhairs are each given breed status. Likewise, the names of colors can change depending on whether you are an American or a British cat owner.

THE IMPORTANCE OF BREED STATUS

The whole question of breed status may not be a matter of any great moment to the owners or breeders in the respective countries cited. Conversely it may be very important. For the average pet owner who simply wants a companion, the standing of a breed may not be influential in his choice, it simply being a question of whether this or that breed is available in his country. To the potential breeder or exhibitor things are rather different.

If a breed has no recognition in your country, then it cannot compete for championship status, and would only be eligible for a limited number of competition classes as Any Other Variety (AOV). If the breed has provisional recognition there will be more classes, but it will still not be able to become a champion. However, that position would probably change after a given period had elapsed, when the breed would ordinarily be upgraded to full recognition, thus championship status. For USA owners (who have a number of registration authorities) a breed that has only limited recognition will only be eligible to compete for championship status with those registrations that accept it.

If a new breed becomes accepted by a given registration body, and is not in any way linked to having genetic weaknesses, it is most probable that in the course of time more registrations will accept it. Eventually, it will gain full competition status. Such breeds offer the newcomer the opportunity to establish themselves firmly in a breed by the time it has gained full recognition. They become an integral part of the breed. This might be preferred to trying to become a top breeder in a long established breed, where obviously the competition will be extremely tough.

I do not suggest that you would want to choose a breed on such grounds, but as there are always new breeds on the horizon, and many of these are very beautiful, it is an aspect that you should at least be aware of so it can be considered in your choice. In the same way, any newcomer to cats should review all of the breeds, because some of the long established ones are not projected as much as are the top cats, such as Persians, Siamese or Burmese. Many of the not-so-popular breeds might offer the newcomer a far better chance of progressing in the breed. This is because the average quality of stock available will tend to be better than in popular breeds.

You are more able to compete with established breeders than is the case in the very popular varieties. You will appreciate from what is discussed in this chapter that selecting a breed is not quite as simple as you might have thought, especially if you plan to become a breeder/exhibitor. Do see as many breeds as you can. Do contact your chosen registration authority in order to find out the standing of the breeds you are interested in.

Feral cats, cats that are allowed to become wild, quickly revert to their instinctive hunting of small rodents, get tabby coloration and become very timid. Photo of a feral cat by Isabelle Francais. The cat is owned by Lucille Adinolfi.

Feline Hair Types

Unlike the situation that pertains to dogs and goldfish, for example, the beauty of a cat is far more dependent on its hair type, its color, and the patterns created by these. Essentially, there are only two basic body forms in the domestic cat, one being the cobby, well built type, the other being the foreign sort, the latter typified by the Siamese. Having decided on the basic body style you prefer, it will be hair type, color, and pattern that will be the deciding factors for you. These aspects are therefore worthy of closer scrutiny.

HAIR TYPES

The coat of the wild cat is of short length, with just a few species exhibiting a somewhat longer coat, but none that compare to the length seen in some domestic breeds. The hair in the latter can be of a number of types as follows: short, medium, long, hairless, Rex, and wire.

Each of these forms, other than the short coat, is the result of mutations to the normal, so we will look first at the latter to see how it is made up.

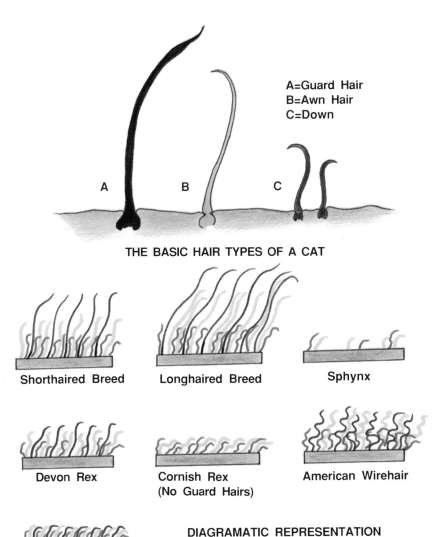

A=Guard Hair
B=Awn Hair
C=Down

THE BASIC HAIR TYPES OF A CAT

Shorthaired Breed

Longhaired Breed

Sphynx

Devon Rex

Cornish Rex
(No Guard Hairs)

American Wirehair

Dense velvet-like
Shortcoat of breeds
like the British Blue

DIAGRAMATIC REPRESENTATION
OF DIFFERING COAT TYPES

THE SHORTHAIR

The length of a short coat is variable, ranging from that seen in breeds such as the Siamese, where it also has little density, to the much more profuse and somewhat longer coat exhibited by breeds such as the Exotic Shorthair, or the average non-purebred shorthair. The coat comprises two types of hair, the top coat and the undercoat, or underfur. The top coat is actually made up of two distinct hair types.

Top Coat: The hair types of this are the guard hairs and the awn or bristle hairs. The guard hairs are the longer of the two, and lay over the awn hairs. The whiskers of a cat, called vibrissae, are also guard hairs, but of a more thick type. There are some of these vibrissae in the body coat. They are thought to be sensory hairs in the same way that the whiskers are. The guard hairs have a slight swelling just below their apex, but overall they show a steady reduction in their diameter from just above the point at which they leave the skin. They thus taper to a fine point at their extremities. Awn hairs are essentially the same as guard hairs, but are slightly shorter and exhibit a corresponding reduction in their thickness and subapical swellings.

The outer surface of the top coat hairs are very smooth and resistant to water, providing they remain independent of each other. Should dirt accumulate on the hairs, the clogging effect this

Chinese Desert Cat, *Felis bieti.*

creates opens gaps and allows water to penetrate to the undercoat, thus to soak the skin. It is for this reason that cats groom themselves fastidiously, and why the longhaired cats must be groomed very regularly.

Undercoat: This comprises shorter hairs, called down, which exhibit a variable amount of crimping. The subapical swelling is absent or virtually so. The hair shaft is almost equal in diameter along its total length. The crimping has the effect of raising the hair from the surface of the body, and keeping the hairs apart from each other. This results in a 'pocket' of warm air, created by the heat of the skin. This is retained to a large degree by the topcoat. The casing of the down hair is softer and more woolly than on the other hair types, so is more able to soak up water should this penetrate the topcoat.

Just how resistant the coat of a cat is to water, cold weather, and sunshine will clearly reflect both its genotype and the quality of its food. The genotype will pass on the ability for the hairs to attain maximum growth and density. The nutrition will provide the amount of proteins, fats, and minerals that will enable the coat's potential to be attained.

If the size and relationship of the three hair types is changed, this will not only affect the visual appearance of the fur. It will also alter its protective properties. This can be shown by considering the other coat types. The medium need not be considered as it will represent a

balance between the short and long coats. Such fur is seen in breeds such as the Birman. It should be added that even in shorthaired cats one can see obvious breeder selection for a reduction in the guard hairs, and an increase in the length of the awn and down hairs. This results in a more velvet-looking plush coat, which is obviously a little less resistant to inclement weather, especially rain, than is the coat which retains its sleek, glossy look. It is also possible to achieve a similar effect by selection for coat density, which will tend to make the hairs stand more upright than would normally be the case. Usually, both of these factors are combined to create the dense, plush coats of breeds such as the Shorthair.

THE LONGHAIR

The mutant gene that creates long hair has not, as far as I know, been studied in great detail in the sense of breeders knowing what its specific effect is. There are two or three possibilities. It could prolong the growth period of the hair, it could increase the growth rate, without prolonging the growth period, or it could be a combination of them both. Further, breeder selection for the natural variation that most genes exhibit will attain the very maximum potential of the mutant gene. If one studies a number of longhaired kittens, it can be very difficult to pinpoint how the gene is working, because some kittens exhibit much fuller coats earlier than do others.

The longhair gene is a recessive in its mode of expression. Its effect is not the same in all breeds. Compare the Persian with the Birman, and these with the Somali, or the Javanese, and you will see what I mean. In the Persian, the length of hair is considerable, in the Birman far less so, and in the other breeds mentioned it is variable, longer on the tail and underbelly than on the back and sides of the body. In the Persian, the guard and awn hairs exhibit a range of properties to the hair shaft. In some, it is quite smooth; in others it is not. This creates the differences that can be found in the texture of the coat within this breed. Some have a much more silky look and feel to them, when compared to those which are more woolly. These differences are historical, and go back to the

HAVANA, CHOCOLATE

PERSIAN, TORTOISESHELL & WHITE

PERSIAN, BLACK & WHITE

PERSIAN, BLACK SMOKE

PERSIAN, BLUE & WHITE

PERSIAN, BLACK

PERSIAN, BLUE SMOKE

JAPANESE BOBTAIL, TORTOISESHELL & WHITE

early days when the more silky haired Angoras were crossed with the more woolly Persians. The down hairs are longer in ratio to the other hairs when compared with the situation in shorthaired breeds. This will tend to increase the woolliness of the coat and make it stand more 'off' from the body.

The standards of Britain and the USA (Cat Fanciers' Association) indicate this situation. The British standard states '...not excessively woolly. Soft and full of life' No mention is made of silkiness. That of the CFA calls for' ...standing off from the body. Of fine texture, glossy...' Producing a glossy coat that stands off from the body is not easy, because silky hair strands are denser than the woolly type, thus will normally lie flatter. However, it is also rather thinner so can be pushed up by a profuse undercoat.

In other breeds there has been an increase in the length of the guard and awn hairs, but not necessarily a corresponding increase in the length of the down hair. The guard hairs have retained a high sheen. This produces the beautiful silky like texture, and more easily managed coats, of the Turkish Van, Angora, and other breeds where the coat is not as long as in the Persian. If a longhaired cat is allowed to go ungroomed, what happens is that dirt binds the hairs of the topcoat and allows water to pass to the underfur. This quickly soaks the down hairs. The dirt binds the hairs together, so a mat is formed. This in turn has the effect of parting the topcoat, thus making it even easier for water to penetrate to the underfur. Eventually, the dirt progresses up the awn and guard hairs, thus covering their polished casing. The end result is a series of large mats which represent the three types of

The world famous cat authority, Richard H. Gebhardt with his American wirehair. Photo by Isabelle Francais.

hairs all bound together, and which are added to by shed hairs that are unable to escape from the tangle. Such a coat will look a very sorry sight. The woolly type Persians are especially prone to mats if their owner is not very diligent about daily grooming.

It can be seen that the short coat of a cat is far less at risk to the sequence of matting that is exhibited by a longer coat. This is because the cat is able to remove both dirt and shedding hairs before they can become coated with debris.

THE HAIRLESS COAT

The hairless condition seen in cats at this time is the result of a recessive gene. Presently, only one example of it is known. It is referred to as the Sphynx, though it is Canadian in origin. The coat is not, in fact, hairless, but there is so little of it that it certainly appears that way, and becomes progressively more bald with age. A few down hairs are produced, and maybe even some awn, but these seem to wither and break away; just a few may remain on the ears and elsewhere. Hairless cats will suffer in all weathers. There cannot be any justification in perpetuating such abnormals, even though the cat appears to suffer no other side effects.

REX HAIR

The rex coat could be said to be a stage towards hairlessness, and some examples of the rex breeds do display areas of very little hair. However, there is no connection between the genes of the rex coat and that for hairlessness. Most rex cats have a full, albeit, very short coat (though a longcoated variety is also now available). There are presently two types of rex, which ironically appeared ten years apart in neighboring counties in the west of England.

The effect of the mutation in the Devon Rex is twofold. Firstly, the hairs do not grow to normal length. Secondly, the guard and awn hairs become crimped, giving the coat its characteristic wavy look. Further, the hairs of the topcoat are more brittle than in normal fur, probably because they exhibit constrictions along their length. These may break at their weakest point. The latter is also very true of the whiskers.

The Cornish Rex does not have the three hair types, the guard hairs being absent. However, the awn hairs retain a high degree of gloss. The effect is a short but very curly and glossy coat. The length of the awn hairs is reduced more so than the down, so they are both about the same size. The rex breeds will obviously be more susceptible to becoming cold or soaked in bad weather, and will also be more at risk to intense sunshine, so owners should bear these facts in mind during extremes of weather. Although only two rex coats are popular there are other rex breeds as the mutation has appeared a number of times over the years.

THE WIRE COAT

The coat of the American Wirehair is a sort of variation on the rex theme. All of the three hair types are present, but grow abnormally. The hairs are thinner, and may be crimped, hooked towards their tip, or bent. The result is an uneven texture to the fur, which does not lie in an even fashion, but stands out from the skin, especially on the body. There may be some reduction in the length of the guard hairs. The mutation, which is dominant in its transmission, is very variable in its effect, so some examples appear much more wiry than others.

One of Richard H. Gebhardt's American wirehairs. Photo by Isabelle Francais.

HIMALAYAN, SEAL POINT

MANX, BROWN CLASSIC TABBY

MAINE COON, BROWN MACKEREL TABBY

MAINE COON, RED CLASSIC TABBY & WHITE

SIAMESE, SEAL POINT

ABYSSINIAN, RUDDY

TONKINESE, NATURAL MINK

PERSIAN, SHADED SILVER

SOMALI, FAWN

RUSSIAN, BLUE

MANX, BLACK & WHITE

ORIENTAL SHORTHAIR, TORTOISESHELL

ORIENTAL SHORTHAIR, BLACK

ORIENTAL SHORTHAIR, FAWN SPOTTED TABBY

PERSIAN, TORTOISESHELL

PERSIAN, SHADED GOLDEN

Coat Colors & Patterns

The range of colors seen in cats today is quite bewildering, though only two basic pigments create these. The actual chemistry of color is beyond the scope of this book, but a brief mention of fundamentals may be useful in creating a background. Color is essentially created by two types of pigment. One is eumelanin, which is brown through black. The other is phaeomelanin, which is yellow through red-orange. The production of these pigments is dependent on the interaction of certain enzymes with amino acids. Although it has not been totally proven, a theory has been advanced that shows how these enzymes may work. It provides a working model. The many interactions are controlled by genes. There are very many of these, in the same way that there are many amino acids that can be oxidized by enzymes to create color. That which follows is very much a simplification.

Imagine an amino acid on which two enzymes work. One we can call A and the other B. The enzyme A is essential for any color to be produced. By itself it creates the yellow-red pigment. Enzyme B has no effect at all by itself, but in the presence of A it results in a dark brown-black pigment. Various genes control not only the presence or absence of the enzymes, but also their strength.

If A and B are at full strength, the result is black. If B is reduced in strength, the result is brown. A further reduction in B produces a lighter brown. If B is absent altogether, the result is yellow-red. If both enzymes are missing, you have an albino. If A is reduced in strength but B is not, the result is gray, the shade being controlled by the relative reduction in the strength of A. If A is virtually nonexistent, but B is present, the result will be almost pure white. Finally, if B is absent, and A is virtually only a trace, you will get an albino, but with some yellowish hues. It will be appreciated that these interactions can produce all possible colors from dense black to white or albino. However, the color is also dependent on other factors.

Cell Construction

A single hair is made up of a central section, called the medulla, surrounded by a layer of cells known as the cortex. Around this is the cuticle, a very thin outer casing of non-living cells. The structure of the cuticle (which is composed of dead cells) determines the relative

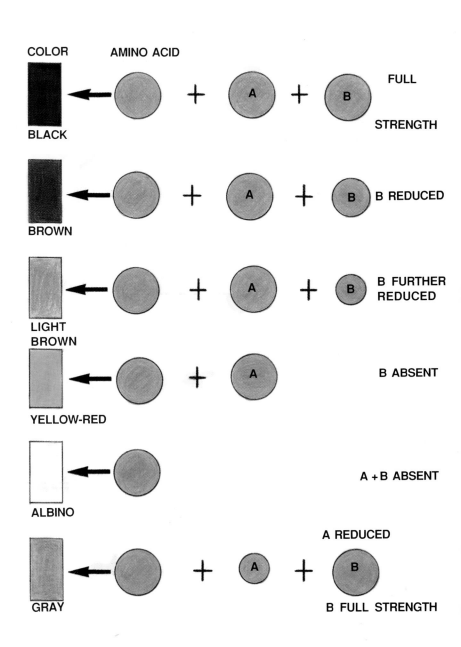

THE CHROMOGEN THEORY PROVIDES A WORKING
MODEL OF COLOR PRODUCTION

amount of sheen the hair displays, and its resistance to water. It also affects our perception of color. However, it is the inner cells that are more important to color. Within the medulla

CROSS-SECTION OF A SINGLE HAIR FIBER

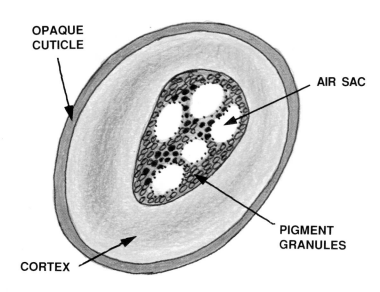

The size of the air sacs will determine the density of the pigment granules.

there are both pigment cells and air sacs. If the cells are packed together they create a darker shade than if they are spaced. Their shape will also affect the color they transmit.

The length and thickness of the hair shaft will also affect the color, because it will create shadows. Finally, the density of the hair, and the color of the underfur, will likewise affect the color projected. There are therefore many factors which combine to produce what we see. Natural mutation of genes has increased the permutations possible, both because they control the enzyme production and because they determine the size and shape of the cells within the hair.

THE EFFECT OF TEMPERATURE

Although for most cats the temperature has little effect on color, in breeds which exhibit the Siamese pattern the temperature is a controlling factor. The Siamese pattern, which is more commonly known in most other animals as the Himalayan, is an example of how the temperature affects the way in which a gene expresses

itself. Put another way, the Siamese color pattern, as such, is not an inherited color in the same way as black or brown is. The Siamese gene permits color to develop up to a certain temperature, beyond which pigment is greatly reduced, and may even be totally absent.

The extremities of the Siamese cat (the face, feet and tail) have a slightly lower temperature than the rest of the body. This allows pigment to be formed. If the temperature is raised, the pigment is reduced, so the cat exhibits a slightly paler color. However, not all cats respond quite the same, because the critical temperature that reduces pigmentation may be higher in some individuals than in others.

To prove that the skin temperature is the controlling factor can be shown by a simple test. If a small amount of hair is removed from the back of a Siamese, and if the cat is placed in a cool room, the new hairs that emerge will be darkly pigmented. As further hairs grow to replace the pigmented hairs that are shed, they will lack pigment, and so the spot will slowly disappear. Conversely, if hairs are removed from the extremities, and the spot covered in some way, this will raise the skin temperature slightly at that spot. The new hairs that grow through will be devoid of pigment, or nearly so. When Siamese kittens are born they do not show their markings because they are kept in a warm environment. The pigment on the ex-

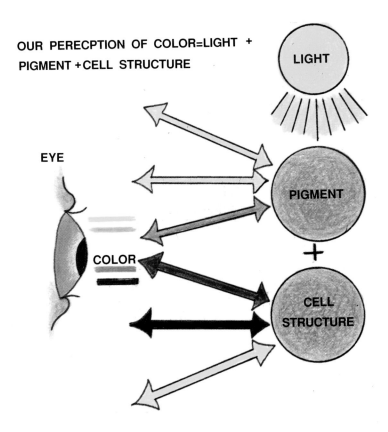

OUR PERECPTION OF COLOR=LIGHT + PIGMENT +CELL STRUCTURE

tremities begins to form later. Were a Siamese kitten to be chilled at birth it would develop pigment over its entire body (assuming the chilling didn't kill it!).

The Siamese gene is recessive in its mode of transmission and is one up in the series from that which totally prevents pigment formation, the albino. However, the latter is not thermo-sensitive, so temperature will not affect the lack of ability for the albino to form pigmentation. A final point worthy of mention in respect of temperature is that, as stated earlier, color in non-Siamese cats is not affected by heat. However, it is affected by sunlight, because certain of the sun's rays have the effect of bleaching pigmentation. The darker the color, the greater the effect, so longhaired black cats will show this effect more than any other color. The result will be that areas of the coat will be brown or brassy in appearance. This of course is the bane of the exhibition owner, so if you live in a hot climate and plan to exhibit, it is worthy of consideration. One must be careful not to confuse bleaching with a poor genetic make-up for the density of a color. In the latter case, protecting the cat from strong sunlight will not result in a better color when new hairs come through.

WILD TYPE COLORATION

In order to appreciate how the various colors and patterns in domestic cats are created it is necessary to consider what the cat's natural color and patterns are. We can commence with the agouti pattern. In this, the pigments are deposited in the hair in the form of bands, the pattern being named for the South American rodent which displays this. It is seen also in wolves, mice, rabbits, guinea pigs, indeed many animals, assumedly because it creates a good camouflage. The actual colors of the banding vary from species to species, but the effect is always the same. It creates a ticking of the fur. Sometimes the base of the hair is black, then there is a brown, red, or yellow band, and finally a yellow or black band. It is the way in which the fur lies that creates the ticking. In small wild cats, a second pattern exists. In this pattern certain groups of hair are heavily pigmented to the tip. The contrast between the areas of

heavily pigmented hairs and those which are tipped with yellow creates the characteristic tabby pattern, as well as the spotted and striped patterns seen in leopards, tigers and other species. There are three forms of tabby striping: 1. The mackerel, which is the wild type. Here, the stripes are, more or less, verti-cal. They may be complete stripes, but are often broken to form bars and spots. 2. The blotched or classic. Here the bands of pigmented hairs are wider and form whorls. The legs usually display more tabby markings than in the mack-erel. 3. Abyssinian. This is the least obvious of the tabbies. The barring is seen on the legs and tail, but the body stripes are barely visible.

The position with regard to spotted cats, such as the British, the Bengal, and the Mau, is not clear. These may be mackerel tabbies in which the vertical stripes have broken up, or they may be an independent gene. If the vertical stripes are broken up, it is the case that breeders have made consistent selection for spots. If there is a separate gene for spotting it would seem to regress if selection is not maintained, because in poor examples the spots coalesce to form variably sized bars or bands.

THE EFFECT OF MUTATIONS

The tabby pattern is basic to all domestic cats, meaning that all cats, regardless of their color or pattern, are obligate tabbies. This fact is often evident in very young kittens that are non-agouti — meaning they exhibit a self (solid) color, or carry two or more colors, but are not visibly tabbies. To better understand this point let us look at a solid black cat and work from this to see how all the other colors are possible.

A mutant gene, representing non-agouti, has the effect of increasing the amount of melanin deposited in the hair cells of those cells which, in the agouti, are yellow, red, or brown. The hair thus looks black. However, the black pigment formed is not quite as dense as in the cells which were black to begin with. For this reason, in the correct light, you can see a faint tracing of the tabby pattern in kittens. This disappears as the kitten grows up, and the density of pigment tends to even out. If you look carefully at the coat of the 'so called' black panther, you

AMERICAN CURL, SEAL LYNX POINT

BURMESE, CHOCOLATE

AMERICAN SHORTHAIR, RED CLASSIC TABBY

AMERICAN SHORTHAIR, SILVER CLASSIC TABBY

JAPANESE BOBTAIL, TORTOISESHELL & WHITE

CORNISH REX, PARTI-COLOR POINT

DEVON REX, BROWN MACKEREL TABBY

DEVON REX, WHITE

will see the spots that show it is a melanistic leopard, or a jaguar, as the case may be, and not a separate species as some people think. Likewise, the young Abyssinian kitten will display faint tabby tracings, though breeders try to select such that these are minimal. In cats where no tracings are seen this may indicate Abyssinian tabby, but not necessarily.

All cats are therefore agouti, in which case they will display a tabby pattern to a greater or

OTHER COAT PATTERNS

Having seen how colors are created, and how they are superimposed over that of the tabby, we can consider a few of the other patterns that are seen in cats.

Shell: In this pattern the very tips of the hair are colored, while the lower part of the hair shaft is a much lighter color.

Shaded: Here, the length of the pigmented area of the hair is greater than in the shell.

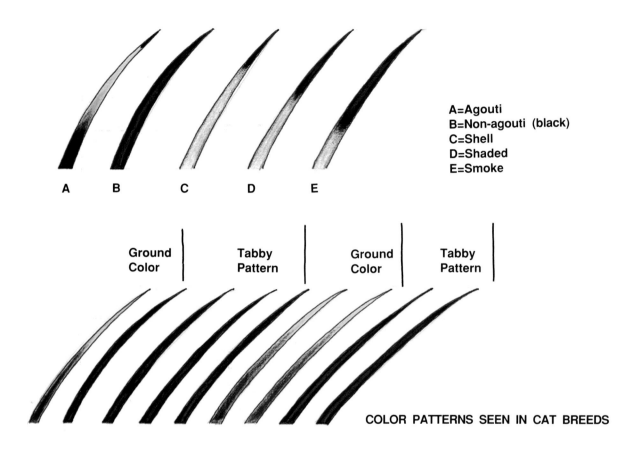

A=Agouti
B=Non-agouti (black)
C=Shell
D=Shaded
E=Smoke

A B C D E

Ground Color | Tabby Pattern | Ground Color | Tabby Pattern

COLOR PATTERNS SEEN IN CAT BREEDS

lesser degree, or they are non-agouti, in which case the agouti and tabby patterns are present, but 'masked' by the extra deposits of melanin in the hairs. If other mutations are present, these will change the black color to something else. For example, the brown mutations will result in a reduction of the black and increase the yellow-brown element of the pigment to create either dark or light brown. The dilute mutation will both reduce the density of the black and spread it more in the cells of the hair to create blue. All of the various mutations therefore act on the non-agouti position. It is of course possible for the agouti, thus tabby, to be present on one part of the cat and not on another, as seen in tabby and whites, and tabby-pointed breeds. In such cases other aspects of genetics come into play, which are beyond the general overview of colors and patterns of this chapter.

Smoke: In this pattern the pigmented area of the hair is greater than in the shaded. When the cat is at rest it appears a more or less uniform color, but once moving the light undercolor can be seen, giving the cat a most beautiful and 'moving' color pattern.

These three variations on a similar theme give rise to a whole range of soft shades seen as the cameo, chinchilla, silver, black and blue smokes and the cameo tabby and others.

Bicolor: This is a two-colored cat. The basis is a color and white. The extent of white on a cat cannot be predicted by breeding, so it can range from a small spot to being an almost white cat with some color markings. From an exhibition standpoint the amount of white is laid down in the standard. The British standard is more specific than its American counterparts in terms of the upper and lower limits of the white and colored areas.

Tortoiseshell: In this pattern the coat comprises various patches of color in yellow and black. The term yellow should be interpreted as ranging from cream to almost red. Nearly all torties are females because the pattern is sex linked.

Calico (Tortoiseshell and white): This is a tortie with the addition of white. Nearly all examples are females because it is a sex-linked color. Contrary to popular belief it is possible to have a male calico, but they are the result of genetic abnormalities, so are very rare.

Blue-Cream: The blue-cream pattern is a tortoiseshell but carrying the dilute mutation that renders the black to blue, and the yellow-red to cream. It is a sex-linked pattern, so only females are seen.

EYE COLOR

The color of a cat's eyes can be any of a range that is probably unequaled in the animal kingdom, excepting perhaps in the order Primates — monkeys and man. As in the coat color, the darker eye colors are created by brown pigments modified by yellow or black, to give the various browns such as hazel, copper and orange, with all of the subtle variations from very light to very dark. To create these colors it is essential that the cells in the iris of the eye contain yellow and brown-black pigments. But how are blue or green eye colors created? As I have never seen this fully explained in a book on cats, it is possibly of interest to readers.

There are no blue or green pigments in a cat, so these colors are the result of optical illusions. Specifically, they are created by Tyndall's phenomenon. When white light is passed through a prism, it is broken into its component parts — these form the colors of the rainbow. Each of the colors represents a differing wavelength. At the short end of these are the blues, while at the long end are yellows through reds.

If the cells in the eye are devoid of eumelanin, the yellow pigment, but contain some dark pigment deeper in the cells, the long wavelengths of light are absorbed, but the short ones, the blues, are not. Because they are short they are deflected back through the air sacs (acting as prisms) in the cells mentioned in

earlier text. Thus you see the reflected blue part of white light. The fact that the cat's eyes are always covered with a film of water no doubt helps this prismatic effect.

The very shortest light wavelengths are in fact violet. Of course, no cats have eyes this color, because the cells in a cat's eyes are not able to absorb all of the lighter blues. But they approach this to a degree in breeds exhibiting deep blue, such as the seal point Birman. The

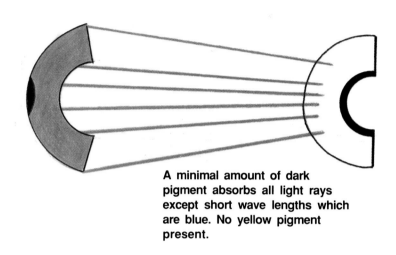

A minimal amount of dark pigment absorbs all light rays except short wave lengths which are blue. No yellow pigment present.

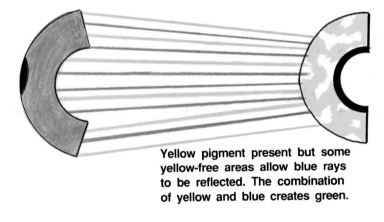

Yellow pigment present but some yellow-free areas allow blue rays to be reflected. The combination of yellow and blue creates green.

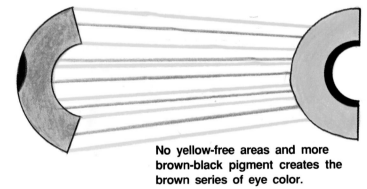

No yellow-free areas and more brown-black pigment creates the brown series of eye color.

EYE COLOR IN CATS
THE THREE BASIC COLOR SERIES IN CATS ARE SHOWN IN THE DIAGRAMS. THE ACTUAL SHADE OF COLOR IS DETERMINED BY THE AMOUNTS OF YELLOW-RED OR BROWN-BLACK PIGMENTS PRESENT.

Cats probably have more varied eye colors than any other living animal.

PERSIAN, TORTOISESHELL

PERSIAN, RED

PERSIAN, RED

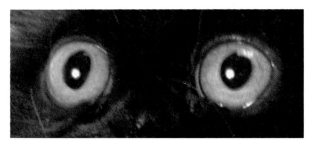

PERSIAN, BLUE SMOKE

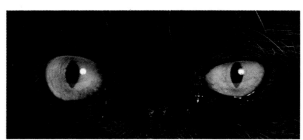

PERSIAN, BLACK

PERSIAN, CREAM & WHITE

PERSIAN, RED CLASSIC TABBY

NORWEGIAN FOREST CAT, BLUE MACKEREL TABBY

SIAMESE, BLUE LYNX POINT

PERSIAN, CHINCHILLA SILVER

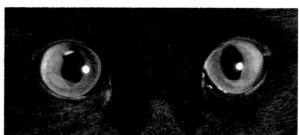

NORWEGIAN FOREST CAT, BLACK

RAGDOLL, SEAL POINT

PERSIAN, BLUE EYED WHITE

SINGAPURA

PERSIAN, SHADED SILVER

ORIENTAL SHORTHAIR, SILVER MACKEREL TABBY

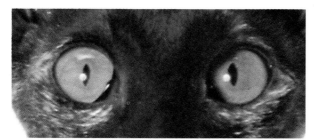

ORIENTAL SHORTHAIR TORTOISESHELL

NORWEGIAN FOREST, BROWN CLASSIC TABBY & WHITE

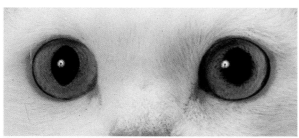

MANX, ODD-EYED WHITE

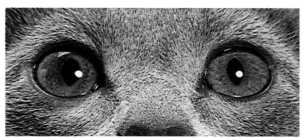

RUSSIAN, BLUE

SCOTTISH FOLD, TORTOISESHELL & WHITE

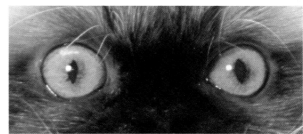

HIMALAYAN, SEAL POINT

NORWEGIAN FOREST CAT, BROWN, MACKEREL, TABBY & WHITE

NORWEGIAN FOREST CAT, BLUE MACKEREL TABBY

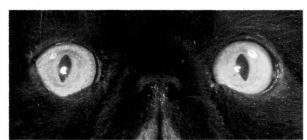

PERSIAN, BLACK

PERSIAN, RED

SCOTTISH FOLD, BLUE MACKEREL

MAINE COON, BROWN CLASSIC TABBY

cheek patches on a budgerigar show the full potential in the dark blue range from Tyndall's phenomenon.

Green is created by there being some yellow pigment in the cells of the iris, but not enough to prevent some light reflection. The yellow pigment combines with the reflected blue light and, as you are aware, blue plus yellow makes green. The shade of green will be determined by two factors. Firstly, the amount of yellow pigment — the less yellow the darker the green. Secondly, the amount of brown-black pigment. As a point of interest, the prime colors in budgerigar feathers — the green and blue series — are the result of this same phenomenon, as is the blue in the sky.

The red and ruby eye color (extremely rare in cats) is created when there is no pigment at all in the iris. It is thus seen in true albinos, and is the hemoglobin of the blood showing through. The nearly yellow color seen in some cat's eyes is created by there being much yellow pigment, very little black, and virtually no light reflecting cells, so very little blue can be seen. This produces what is actually an extremely light green.

The relationship of eye to body color can only be expressed in rather vague terms. Dark colored cats will invariably have dark colored eyes within the range of that eye color, and vice versa. White and light colored coats will normally have an eye color of blue or light green. However, there are so many exceptions to such generalizations, especially in the darker colors, that one is bound to conclude that eye color is controlled by a whole complex of factors, of which some will relate to the colors carried in the coat. Although I have never seen any data in respect of characters linked to eye color (deafness in blue-eyed whites apart) there is some data from studies made in dogs (Greyhounds and German Shepherd Dogs). This suggests that eye color is linked to intelligence, the lighter eye being associated with greater intelligence. There is also evidence that when the dilution gene is present this will affect eye color. As cats are never bred or tested for intelligence, such linkage may be of no importance, but it is an interesting aspect given that many standards prefer a darker shade of eye color (which is also true of most dog breeds).

The apparent color of a cat's eyes will, of course, be influenced by the color of the surrounding fur. A light-colored eye will appear to be much lighter if on a dark faced cat than if exactly the same color was surrounded by fur of a lighter hue. The reverse is also true.

THE NAMES OF COLORS

The names used in the cat fancy to describe the colors exhibited by cats are numerous. Some are very obvious and easily identified. Others are much less so. While most are applied by all registrations in all countries, a few are given alternative names in different associations. Some are used exclusively in a single breed. Here, all of the names currently in use in Great Britain and the USA are listed, together with their alternative names. Descriptive comments are given where deemed necessary. The list is alphabetical for ease of reference, but is cross-referenced where two or more names are in use for the same color.

Color is a very subjective matter, so that what one person might regard as golden, frost, or cream may not be held as such by another. A color noted on a pedigree written shortly after the birth of a litter could have changed by the time the kitten has matured. Color is never final, and changes steadily with maturity, especially in those colors that are shades of a basic color, such as brown.

The number of names in the list should not be taken to indicate a separate genetic base for each name. Many have the same genotype, but with numerous names applied to them. Others represent breeder selection for the variability of a gene towards the lighter or darker ends of that variation. In the list I have cited a number of names which are not colors per se. They are composites of colors — such as Usual and Tawny for example. All colors can be combined with coat patterns; thus you can have a blue smoke, a silver tabby, a shaded golden and so on.

Black: This is the most commonly used name but Ebony is used in the Oriental Shorthair. Blue: This is not a true blue but more a gray color: it is the dilution of black.

Bronze: This term is used in the Egyptian

Mau of the USA. It covers a range of brown shades that make up the color.

Brown: A seal brown used in the Burmese of the UK as well as in numerous tabby breeds. It should be pointed out that in tabbies the brown refers to the ground color, so the brown tabby's markings are in fact black.

Caramel: A shade of buffish brown.

Champagne: Warm honey beige. Used in USA in the Burmese. Its UK equivalent is Chocolate,

Chestnut: Rich brown. Used in the Oriental Shorthair of the USA.

Chocolate: A warm milk chocolate brown. See also Champagne. Also described as chestnut brown in some standards.

Cinnamon: A light reddish brown. The dilution of non-sex linked red.

Cream: This is the dilution of Red. It ranges from very pale to almost red. It may be termed buff cream.

Ebony: Black. Used in the Oriental Shorthair of the USA.

Fawn: Various shades of brown.

Frost: An alternative to Lilac.

Golden: An apricot color that becomes golden on the topcoat.

Havana: Used only in the breed of that name. A chestnut or mahogany brown.

Honey: A light to medium honey brown. See Mink.

Lavender: An alternative to Lilac used in numerous breeds, especially in the USA.

Lilac: A frost gray with pinkish tone (USA); a dove gray with pinkish cast (UK). It is the dilution of chocolate. Also seen as Frost (USA), and Lavender (UK).

Mink: This termed is used exclusively in the Tonkinese and is prefixed by natural, honey, champagne and platinum. It actually also re-fers to coat quality as well as color.

Platinum: A pale silver gray with pale fawn undertones. Used in the Burmese of the USA. Its alternative is Lilac.

Red: Is more an orange than a red, and very variable from light to dark. It is a sex-linked

Hang in there, Kitty. Cats have a unique sense of balance. A dog couldn't do this! Photo by Robert Pearcy.

color, so its use in the Abyssinian breed is misleading as this latter color is a recessive and not sex-linked. The dilute of true red is cream, but the dilute of Abyssinian red is fawn. See also Sorrel.

Ruddy: In the USA a ruddy brown or burnt sienna ticked with black. It equates Usual of the UK. Only used in the Abyssinian.

Sable: Used in the USA in the Burmese. It equates to Seal.

Seal: A dense brown. Seen in pointed breeds such as Siamese and Birman. Called Brown in the Burmese of the UK.

Silver: Variable from pale to dark.

Sorrel: A red ticked with brown and used solely in the Abyssinian of the UK. Its American equivalent is Red.

Tawny: Black or brown spotting on ruddy or bronze ground. Used only in the Ocicat of the USA.

Usual: A rich golden brown ticked with black. Used in the Abyssinian. Called Ruddy in the USA.

Domestic Cat Classification

If you are a first-time purebred cat owner you may, depending on in which country you live and which registration body you choose to support, experience a greater or lesser degree of difficulty in understanding the domestic classification of the breeds. This situation is brought about by the fact that in cats, unlike in dogs, rabbits, budgerigars and many other popular pets, there is invariably more than one registration body in a given country. The result, from a purely outside-observer's viewpoint, is that this makes it much more difficult to understand classifications.

In reviewing the manner in which the breeds are presented by differing organizations, that of the Cat Fanciers' Association (CFA) of the USA represents the simplest system. Here the breeds are presented in alphabetical order. Each color within the breed is a variety of that breed. The American Cat Association (ACA) is an example of the next logical step in breed division. Here the breeds are divided into long-haired and shorthaired, the colors being divided into divisions, such as the solid colors, the shaded, the smokes, the tabbies and so on.

Rather more complex is the system used by The International Cat Association (TICA)of the USA. Here the breeds are divided into five categories: Established, Newer Natural, Variant or Mutational, Hybrids, and Experimental breeds. It is hardly ideal because obvious hybrids and mutational breeds appear in the Established list, while long established breeds appear in the Newer Natural list. The system is thus ambiguous in its framework.

The height of complexity is seen in the system of Britain's Governing Council of the Cat Fancy (GCCF). Here the breeds are housed in six basic groups. However, we find the Exotic Shorthair in the longhaired group, while the Angora is classed as an Oriental Shorthair. The term Persian, dropped in former standards, has now been reinstated in a loose fashion. Each color within the Persians and other breeds is given breed status. All breeds, and the colors in them, are given a number. The number system is a very cumbersome area for anyone trying to make sense of it. The GCCF is a fine registration body with excellent policies in respect of its stand against accepting deformed breeds into its ranks. However, its classification of the breeds is antiquated and in need of total revision and better presentation that will make it more straightforward for the average cat owner to follow.

The fact that there are differing registration bodies in the USA, the UK, and Australia creates many complications for the average breeder/exhibitor. The standards of the breeds differ slightly, as do exhibition rules. The names applied to colors may change from one body to the next, as might the acceptance of a number of breeds. The apparent answer would be if the clubs were to unite and form a single representative body, as in dogs. However, such monopolies, while giving more stability to color terms and standards, are not always able to represent the views and needs of all of those involved in the fancy, so the problem is not easily overcome.

BREED DETERMINATION

In the previous three chapters various aspects of importance in breed definition have been discussed. We can now look at the fundamental ways in which breeds are classified without specific reference to individual registration associations. This will give you a better overview of domestic cat classification.

Cats can be broadly divided into those which have long hair and those with short hair. There are a few breeds which might be termed midway situations, but these are invariably regarded as longhaired breeds. Examples would be the Birman, the Ragdoll and the Somali. As a rule of thumb you can assume that any breed that is not obviously shorthaired will be classed as a longhair. Within these two hair types there are then further types based on body conformation. We will consider them within the framework of the hair types.

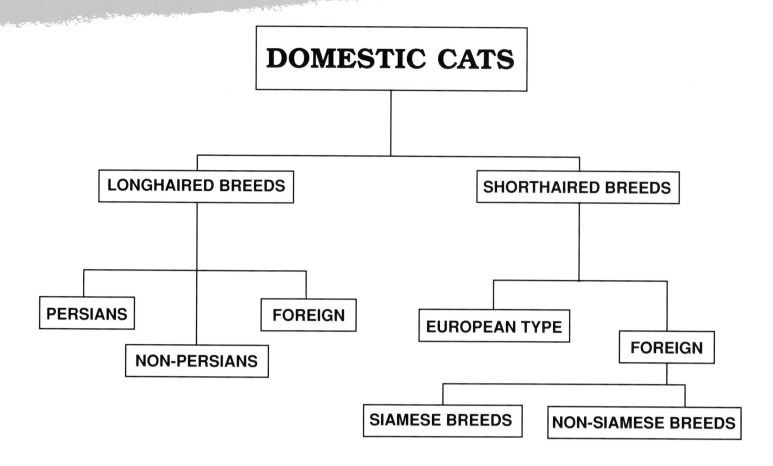

The Basic Classification of Domestic Cats

Longhaired Breeds

The longhairs can be divided into three broad types. The first is the Persian, the second might be termed the non-Persian, while the third is the foreign. The Persian has a cobby sort of body, but is distinguished by its very long hair. The non-Persians are a collection of breeds in which the hairlength varies from quite long to medium. These breeds have powerful well muscled bodies and well defined muzzles. The term 'foreign' applied to the third group does not refer to the country of origin, but to the body type. These breeds are of a slender build, with a head shape that is more or less similar to that of the Siamese, though not quite as wedge-shaped when viewed from the front. The longhaired breeds can thus be grouped as follows:

1. **Persians** in their many color varieties, and including the Himalayan and Kashmir, which are given separate breed status in some associations.
2. **Non Persians:** American Curl; Angora; Birman; Cymric; Maine Coon; Norwegian Forest; Ragdoll; Siberian; Tiffany; Turkish Van.
3. **Foreign:** Balinese; Javanese; Nebelung; Oriental Longhair; Somali.

Shorthaired Breeds

The shorthaired breeds can be divided into two basic groups (possibly even three). The first are what might be termed the European type. These are solid cobby cats displaying good size of bone and round faces. Their eye shape is essentially just slightly ovoid. The second group are the foreigns. These have a slender build and finer bone. Many, though by no means all, have a more or less wedge-shaped face. The archetypal foreign is, of course, the Siamese. The eye shape ranges from ovoid to an obvious oriental slant. The various breeds in these two categories are as follows:

1. **British or European Types:** American Curl; American Shorthair; American Wirehair; Bengal; British Shorthair; California Spangled; Chartreux; Exotic Shorthair; Manx; Scottish Fold.
2. **Foreign:** Abyssinian; Bombay; Burmese; Chinese Harlequin; Copper; Cornish Rex; Devon Rex; Egyptian Mau; Havana; Japanese Bobtail; Korat; Ocicat; Oriental Shorthair; Russian Blue; Siamese; Singapura; Snowshoe; Sphynx; Tonkinese.

It can be seen at a glance that there are about

twice as many shorthaired breeds as there are longhairs. This is not surprising because the natural hair of the cat is short. The longhaired gene has been steadily introduced to shorthaired breeds via the Persian to create a longhaired equivalent of the shorthair, which gains breed status, or to create new breeds. Alternatively, a gene for long hair has appeared in a shorthaired breed independent of that from the Persian. Presently, the longhaired equivalents to existing shorthaired breeds are as follows:

The Balinese is a longhaired Siamese.

The Cymric is a longhaired Manx.

The Nebelung is a longhaired Russian Blue.

The Somali is a longhaired Abyssinian.

The Tiffany is a longhaired Burmese.

In the coming years we shall no doubt see more longhaired equivalents to shorthaired breeds because it is presently very fashionable to try and create new breeds of all types. Some will catch on, but most will be destined to remain in obscurity.

NON PUREBRED CATS

While your interest in this book may revolve around the fact that you are thinking of having an established breed, this may not necessarily be so. Many potential catowners like to look at the numerous breeds, yet settle for a non-purebred, or moggie-type cat, as they are affectionately called. For one thing, the moggie will cost you substantially less than the purebred. Further, the basic gene pool in cats is small compared to that in dogs. This means that all(!) cats have nice proportions and are well marked in terms of their patterns and colors. Indeed, some are quite stunning, and more beautiful than many of the established breeds. The genes of possibly a number of breeds have combined in their make-up to produce a gorgeous feline.

The majority of moggies will be one of five basic sorts. There will be tabbies, tortoiseshells, bicolors, whites and blacks. Both long and shorthaired, mostly shorthaired, will be seen in these patterns and colors. Some will have the British or American shorthair look to them, while others will reflect their foreign ancestry — usually stemming from a Siamese Romeo out-on-the-tiles-type!

BREED POPULARITY

Trying to gauge the popularity of breeds on a global basis is at this time virtually an impossibility. The reasons are two fold. First, there are some seven registration associations in the USA, and two in the UK. Many breeders are registered with two or more associations, so multiple registrations are common. Secondly, not all associations use computers to record registrations, and appear not to be able to produce breakdowns of the registrations, breed by breed. This is surprising, given that the kennel clubs of the world were able to give breed breakdowns of registrations, by breed, decades before computers came into use.

Fortunately, the world's largest cat registry, the CFA, has issued figures for years, so I have reproduced a popularity chart based on its figures for the year 1987. This represents a guide to the relative popularity of the breeds. If a breed is not included in the list it is because the CFA did not in that year recognize it. Were the figures for Great Britain to be known and included, there is no doubt at all that certain breeds, such as the British Shorthair, the Burmese, and the Birman, would move to a higher chart position. However, until such a time comes when other associations are able to compile lists, the one included is at least a start. If hair types are considered, then in the USA the longhaired breeds are much more popular in relation to overall registrations than they are in the UK. In the CFA they accounted for 78.4% of all registrations in the year stated. In the UK they made up only 40.3% of the total. Siamese are about four times more popular in the UK (relative to all registrations) than they are in the USA, while the Burmese is about nine times more popular in the UK than in the USA, again, relative to the total registrations of these two major associations.

CAT BREED
POPULARITY CHART
*(Reproduced by courtesy of the
Cat Fanciers Association, Inc.)*

Breed	Registrations
Persian	52,633
Siamese	3,656
Abyssinian	2,367
Maine Coon	1,852
Burmese	1,233
Oriental Shorthair	1,080
American Shorthair	1,034
Exotic Shorthair	887
Scottish Fold	820
Colorpoint Shorthair	761
Birman	720
Cornish Rex	589
Manx	557
Russian Blue	516
Balinese	498
Somali	411
Tonkinese	359
Ocicat	336
British Shorthair	284
Devon Rex	204
Egyptian Mau	195
Norwegian Forest	161
Japanese Bobtail	149
Javanese	141
Chartreux	98
Korat	93
Angora	88
Bombay	83
Havana	81
American Curl	73
Singapura	44
American Wirehair	29

ABYSSINIAN

HISTORY: Clouded in myths and tales, the Abyssinian is said to have been taken to England from Ethiopia (formerly Abyssinia) by British troops and travelers. The child of the gods, it is said to have direct links to the cats of the pharaohs, thus to their cat goddesses. While there may be some truth in the fact that cats were taken from the Middle East to Britain, all the evidence points to the Aby being the product of British breeders. Most of the early Abys were silver ticked and tabby, rather than the red, which they are most famed as. The first registered cats in the UK appeared in 1896. Both were of unknown parentage. Matings between British shorthairs and, probably, some imported cats of African ticked-type, helped to establish the agouti pattern and reduce the extent of tabby markings.

ABYSSINIAN, SORREL
Female, Grand Champion
Eleven months old

The breed arrived in the USA about 1906 in the form of Aluminum 11, and Salt, who were sired by Aluminum out of Fancy Free, two of the most important British Abys in the breed's early history.

ALLOWABLE OUTCROSSES: None.

RECOGNITION: All associations.

DESCRIPTION

Head: With a natural appearance the Aby head, in profile, has the look of a miniature mountain lion. Gentle slope from nose to forehead. The frontal view of the head is of a soft wedge, 73 neither round nor Siamese in shape.

Ears: Set wide apart, broad at base, and tapering to a rounded tip. Ideally, tufted with hair.

Eyes: Almond shaped; amber, hazel or green in color. A light eye color is undesirable. Eyes highlighted by narrow circle of light-colored fur.

Body: Of foreign type, the body is long, lithe and muscular. Cobbyness or Siamese types are too undesirable. Proportions more important than size. Cat is of medium stature.

Legs & Feet: Slim legs of good length. Feet small and oval.

Tail: Thick at base, fairly long and tapering.

Coat: Short, but sufficiently long for the hairs to accommodate two or three bands of ticking. Dense and of a high sheen, the fur is also soft and silky to the touch.

Color: The long established colors are:

Usual (UK) or Ruddy (USA)	Golden brown ticked with dark brown and/or black. Paw pads Black, nose leather brick red.

ABYSSINIAN, RUDDY
Male, Kitten

Sorrel (UK) or Red (USA)	Copper or rich red, ticked with chocolate, Base hair apricot. Paw pads and nose leather pink.
Blue	Soft blue-gray ticked with slate or steel blue. Base hair oatmeal (cream to beige). Paw pads mauvish-blue, nose leather dark pink.

Some associations only accept the given colors but others (e.g., GCCF) accept silver, chocolate, lilac, fawn (dilute sorrel), Red (sex linked), cream, and torties in all the colors listed. The silver Aby is an especially beautiful feline.

ABYSSINIAN, SORREL
Female, Novice
Eight months old

ABYSSINIAN, RUDDY
Female, Kitten

ABYSSINIAN, "RED"
Female, Grand Champion

ABYSSINIAN, BLUE
Male

Bad Faults: Bars on legs, chest and tail (but ghost markings often seen in kittens), kinked or whip tail, extremes of type, wrong eye color, white lockets and white that extends beyond lips to the neck.

Remarks: The Abyssinian, though not a natural breed, could easily convince you it was in its red ticked colors. It is a very popular breed in the USA and only a little less so in Great Britain. A connoisseur's cat that will gain more popularity with the establishment of the newer colors.

ABYSSINIAN, RUDDY
Female

ABYSSINIAN, RUDDY
Neutered male, Double Grand Champion
Two years and nine months old

AMERICAN CURL

HISTORY: The curl mutation, which is the basis of this breed, was first noted in California in 1981. It was seen in a female called Shulamith, who is thus the founding queen of the breed. The early American Curls were both long and shorthaired, so both are breeds. The unusual Curl breed gained recognition from TICA in 1985. It has steadily increased its numbers since then. The mutation is transmitted as a simple dominant, which means that when a curl cat is mated to a non curl, there is a 50% chance of producing a curl kitten. When two of these curl cats are paired the chances of curl kittens increases to 75%.

AMERICAN CURL, SEAL LYNX POINT
Male
Nine months old

RECOGNITION: TICA.

DESCRIPTION

Head: Moderate in size and round when viewed from the front. There is not a well defined break (stop), the nose showing a gentle rise to the forehead.

Ears: Relatively large and wide at the base. Firm to the touch, they display varying degrees of backward curl — revealing the inner surface of the outer ear, or trumpet.

Eyes: Large and round but with a very slight angle. This may not be apparent in many examples.

Body: Medium in size, and neither cobby nor svelte.

Legs & Feet: Moderate in length and bone, the legs are well muscled, and the feet are compact and round.

Tail: The length of the tail should be the same as that from shoulders to the base of the tail.

Coat: The shorthaired American Curl has a coat of even length. Its is dense and lies flat to the body. It should possess a healthy sheen. The longhaired American Curl has minimal underfur so it lies flat to the body. It is silky to the touch and of moderate length with no neck ruff. The ears are well furnished with hair. The tail fur is generous and plum-like in appearance.

Color: The range of colors and their patterns is extensive. It includes all of those which are popular in most other breeds. The eye, paw pads, and nose leather should be of a color that is appropriate to the body color(s).

Bad Faults: Kink in tail, cobbyness, foreign type, woolly hair, ears that are not erect, or firm to the touch, or matched with each other.

AMERICAN CURL, BLACK (SHORTHAIRED)
Female

AMERICAN CURL, BLACK
Female

AMERICAN CURL, BROWN MACKEREL
TABBY AND WHITE
Male
Five months old

AMERICAN CURL, BLUE
Female, Kitten
Four months old

Remarks: The American Curl is an attractive breed. Obviously the backward curling ears will be more prone to problems than those of breeds with normal ears. They must be inspected on a very regular basis to ensure they remain clean and free from parasitic attack. In all other aspects the breed is delightful.

AMERICAN CURL, BLACK AND WHITE
Male

AMERICAN SHORTHAIR

HISTORY: British and European shorthaired cats accompanied the Pilgrim fathers and other settlers to the New England states. These were tough felines well able to cope with the climate and the rodents native to the USA. They were the working and street cats, so when cat showing became the 'in' thing no one really gave them much thought. However, a registry was started. The first name to be enrolled was Belle — a ginger tom from England. More English cats followed, imported by Jane Cathcart (who was also the first importer of Abyssinians). These were mated with local cats. Buster Brown became the first registered homebred 'shorthair,' as they were then called.

By the 1960s the term *domestic* had long been added. At this time the breed really started to take off. However, some Americans wanted a more glamorous shorthair, so many Persians were hybridized with the Domestic Shorthair. This created a controversy that ultimately resulted in the creation of the Exotic Shorthair, while the Domestic Shorthair, to be renamed the American Shorthair in 1965, returned to its grass-roots type. A hint of the Persian can still be seen in some American Shorthair faces. Some registries still accept street cats that fulfill the requirements of the standard in order to ensure retention of the breed's basic qualities. Others disagree with this practice on the grounds that the existing gene pool is large enough to ensure this will be so.

ALLOWABLE OUTCROSSES: None.

RECOGNITION: All American associations.

DESCRIPTION

Head: Medium to large (depending on the association). The full cheeks give a wide expression to the face. Neck powerful as befits a cat well able to hunt and look after itself. Soft break from the shortish wide nose to the rounded forehead. Viewed from front there is no dome to the skull.

Ears: Of moderate size, certainly never too large. Rounded at tip. Excessive furnishings of inner ear trumpet undesirable. Width between ears to be about twice the distance between the eyes.

Eyes: Large and round (GCCF), large and wide with upper lid almond shaped (CFF), or oval (ACA). Most other associations prefer large and round. Tendency to oriental shape a fault.

AMERICAN SHORTHAIR, RED CLASSIC
TABBY

Body: Powerful and cobby in shape, the back is straight, the shoulders, rump and chest broad. Of medium to large size the breed must never look rangy.

Legs & Feet: Straight and of medium length — somewhat longer than in the British Shorthair. Well muscled. Feet round, with heavy pads.

Tail: Of medium length, thick base, and tapering to a rounded tip.

Coat: Short, dense, and even in length. Harsh or crisp to the touch but with lustrous sheen. Silky and overlong coats are decided faults.

Color: There are in excess of thirty color coat patterns seen in the American Shorthair. A number of the more popular colors are shown herewith:

AMERICAN SHORTHAIR, BLACK
Female
Three years and six months old

AMERICAN SHORTHAIR, RED CLASSIC TABBY
Male, Grand Champion

White: Pure and untinged with yellow. Markings: None. Eyes: Blue-deep sapphire, or brilliant gold, odd-eyed (one blue one gold). Paw Pads & Nose Leather: Pink.

Black: Dense coal black. Markings: None. Eyes: Copper, orange, or brilliant gold. Paw Pads: Black or brown. Nose Leather: Black.

Blue: Light to medium (the lighter shades preferred in the USA). Markings: None. Eyes: Brilliant gold. Paw Pads & Nose Leather: Blue.

Red: Deep rich red without shading, markings or ticking (CFA). Markings: None. Eyes: Brilliant gold. Paw Pads & Nose Leather: Brick red.

Cream: Buff cream (CFA). Markings: None. Eyes: Brilliant gold. Paw Pads & Nose Leather: Pink.

Bicolor: White with unbrindled patches of color (CFA). Colors include: black/white, blue/white, red/white, and cream/white. Eyes: Brilliant gold. Paw Pads and Nose Leather: Pink and/or the color.

The Van bicolors are the same but the color is confined to the extremities of head tail and legs as in the Turkish Van breed.

TABBY PATTERN

Either the classic (blotched) or mackerel, the blotched being much more popular. The favorite colors are:

Brown Tabby: Brown ground color with black markings. Eyes: Brilliant gold. Paw Pads: Black or Brown. Nose Leather: Brick red.

Blue Tabby: Bluish ivory ground with darker blue markings. Eyes: Brilliant gold. Paw Pads: Rose. Nose Leather: Old rose.

Red Tabby: Red ground color with deep rich red markings. Eyes: Brilliant copper. Paw Pads & Nose Leather: Brick red.

Silver Tabby: Pale, clear silver ground color with black markings. Eyes: Green or hazel. Paw pads and Nose Leather: Brick red.

Cream Tabby: Very pale cream ground color with darker cream markings that should be dark enough to be distinct.

Patched Tabby: Also known as Torbie, this is a tabby which has patches of red and/or cream. There are silver, brown, or blue patched tabbies.

OTHER COLOR PATTERNS

Calico (Tortoiseshell and white in UK): White with unbrindled patches of black and red. Eye color is brilliant gold. The dilute Calico has markings in blue and cream.

AMERICAN SHORTHAIR, SILVER CLASSIC
TABBY
Male

AMERICAN SHORTHAIR, SHADED

Male, Champion

AMERICAN SHORTHAIR, BROWN CLASSIC
TABBY
Male, Champion

AMERICAN SHORTHAIR, SILVER CLASSIC
TABBY
Male

AMERICAN SHORTHAIR, SHADED SILVER
Female, Triple Grand Champion

Chinchilla: Most of the hair is pure white. There is just enough black tipping to the hair, especially on the back and sides, to create a silver appearance. Eyes: Green or blue-green. Paw Pads: Black. Nose Leather: Brick red.

Shaded Silver: The same as the Chinchilla but with more of the hair containing black pigment to create a darker shade.

AMERICAN SHORTHAIR, SILVER CLASSIC
TABBY
Female, Kitten

AMERICAN SHORTHAIR, SILVER CLASSIC
TABBY
Male, Champion

Shell Cameo: This is a Chinchilla pattern but in red. Likewise, the shaded cameo is the darker version of this. Eyes: Brilliant gold. Paw Pads & Nose Leather: Rose.

Smokes: In this pattern there is even more pigment in the hairs. Only the very base hair is white so is only seen when the cat moves. The colors are either black, blue, or red.

Bad Faults: Any suggestion of hybridization, such as long or woolly hair, deep stop or nose break, or bulging eyes. Kink in tail, incorrect colored eyes and any white lockets on a color not specifying such.

Remarks: The American Shorthair has come a long way from its humble origins yet should remain a cat capable of surviving on its own if the need arose. They make excellent pets for those who want a cat that is undemanding yet can be very affectionate. The tabby pattern is seen at its best in shorthaired breeds such as this.

AMERICAN WIREHAIR

HISTORY: The mutation that created this breed occurred in a litter of farm cats in Verona, New York, in 1966. The effect of the mutation is that the hairs become crimped and hooked. This produces a harsh lamb's-wool-type feel to the coat. All three hair types (guard, awn and down) are present. The original mutant cats were of unknown type but were shorthaired. The breed has not gained the popularity of the other Rex-type breeds but enjoys a small but steady following. The mutation is of the dominant type, which means that when a wirehair is paired to an American Shorthair, or any other breed, there will be a 50% chance that wirehaired kittens will be produced.

ALLOWABLE OUTCROSSES: American shorthair.

RECOGNITION: CFA: TICA.

DESCRIPTION

Head: Round, with prominent cheekbones. The muzzle is well developed.

Ears: Of medium size, set well apart, and with rounded tips.

Eyes: Large and round. Aperture has a slight upward tilt.

Body: Medium to large in size, but proportions more important than actual size. Level back, with shoulders and hips of the same width. Generally, a well-muscled cat of American Shorthair type.

Legs & Feet: Medium in length and bone, but with good covering muscle. Paws oval and compact.

Tail: Neither overlong nor unduly short, the base is thick and tapers to a rounded tip.

Coat: The main feature of the breed. It is of medium length, springy and coarse. Each hair is crimped, hooked or bent, with no relationship to other hairs. While the overall effect is the same, there is much variety exhibited within the coat of any one individual. Ringlet, rather than waves, is the desired effect. Curly whiskers are desirable, though not common.

Color: Any color acceptable in the American Shorthair is allowed in the Wirehair. You are therefore referred to that breed for details of colors, eye color, and that of paw pads and nose leather.

Bad Faults: A deep nose break, kinked tail, or long and fluffy fur. Any suggestion of hybridization that results in the colors chocolate or lilac, or in the Himalayan pattern, would result in disqualification in an exhibition American Wirehair.

Remarks: An interesting breed that will have appeal to those liking a hardy and undemanding breed that is just a little different from the average shorthair, without taking matters to extremes. The mutation creating the coat type has no recorded adverse side effects.

AMERICAN WIREHAIR, CALICO
Female

BALINESE/JAVANESE

HISTORY: The Balinese is a longhaired Siamese. The mutant gene that created the longhair appeared in a litter of Siamese kittens during the late 1940s or early 1950s. By the 1960s the breed was appearing in shows as Any Other Variety (AOV), and quickly gained devotees on account of its graceful lines. By 1970 it had gained full recognition with all of the American registries, but had to wait until the late 1980s before gaining championship status in Great Britain.

A Javanese (recognized as a separate breed by CFA), is a Balinese in any other color or pattern other than seal, blue, chocolate or lilac. Javanese initially resulted from crosses between Balinese and related breeds.

Its named is derived from the fact that Helen Smith, an early pioneer in the breed, felt that it resembled the dancers from Bali in its grace and movement. Certainly the name Balinese is more attractive than its original name of Long-haired Siamese.

Although most registries accept the breed in many colors, the CFA does not. In the CFA registry only the original Siamese colors are permitted, all others being regarded as a separate breed — the Javanese.

ALLOWABLE OUTCROSSES: Siamese.

RECOGNITION: All associations.

DESCRIPTION

Head: Long and forming a triangle from the nose to the tips of the ears. When seen in profile the nose must be straight, with no dips along its length. Strong chin and level bite.

Ears: Large and pointed at their tips. They must have good width at their base.

Eyes: Oriental or almond shaped and sloping towards the nose. They should be neither protruding nor sunken. The apparent shape of the eyes will vary according to the light intensity and the mood of the cat. Sometimes they will appear more almond shaped than at other times. Eye color is deep vivid blue (CFA) or bright clear blue (GCCF).

Body: Medium sized, lithe yet muscular. The hips should never be wider than the shoulders. The Siamese type is less obvious in the Balinese because the fur gives the breed a more solid look.

Legs & Feet: Rear legs slightly higher than those of the front. They should be slim and elegant, never looking too stocky. Feet are small and oval shaped. Five toes on front feet and four on rear.

JAVANESE, BLUE LYNX POINT
Female

Tail: Long, straight and tapering. Free of any indication of a kink.

Coat: Of medium length, fine, silky and lying flat to the body. Although some underfur will be present, the standards on both sides of the Atlantic require 'without woolly or downy undercoat'. The tail fur is plume-like. The absence of a frill of fur on the face is to be preferred. The coat of this breed does not fully develop until the cat is mature.

Color: The color of the points, being the face (mask), ears, feet and tail, should ideally be of the same shade, and clearly defined from the color of the body. The contrast will be more obvious in the darker colors than in the lighter shades. The permitted colors are:

CFA: Seal Point: Body pale fawn to cream. Pads seal. Chocolate Point: Body ivory. Pads cinnamon pink. Blue Point: Body bluish white. Pads slate color. Lilac Point: Body glacial white. Pads lavender pink.

GCCF and most USA Associations : Seal, blue, chocolate, lilac, red, cream, tortie, and tabby in all colors. Generally, any color accepted in Siamese will be permitted in the Balinese.

Bad Faults: White toes, kink in tail, cross eyes, lack of pigment on pads or nose leather, uneven bite, non-blue eyes, and an obvious woolly underfur.

Remarks: This very attractive breed will clearly appeal to those who like the Siamese — but also longhaired breeds. The coat is very manageable, a decided advantage with any longhaired cat, a fact reflected in the growing popularity of this breed.

JAVANESE, SEAL LYNX POINT

JAVANESE, SEAL LYNX POINT
Female, Champion

BALINESE, LILAC LYNX POINT
Female

BENGAL

HISTORY: The Bengal is one of a number of relatively recent arrivals on the cat scene that has still to gain worldwide recognition. Its progress has been considerably better than that of the California Spangle, though like the Spangle, it is still a very expensive cat. The breed came into being during the 1980s. It is said to be a cross between the Asiatic leopard cat, *Felis bengalensis*, and domestic shorthairs. The result is a wild-looking feline that, happily, does not display the unbridled ferocity of its wild ancestor.

ALLOWABLE OUTCROSSES: As a developing breed, there are no restrictions on the breeding programs for this breed, though Bengal-to-Bengal is obviously the preferred mating.

RECOGNITION: TICA.

DESCRIPTION

Head: Large and round. The muzzle and nose are medium-short. There is no stop, the nose meeting the forehead at a slight angle.

Ears: Medium to large, erect, and placed well up on the head. With a wide base they taper to a rounded tip.

Eyes: Large and round. Green or amber in color.

Body: Long, tubular and muscular.

Legs & Feet: Proportionate to the body, they are muscular, straight and of medium length. Those of the front are as long as those of the back, or even shorter. The paws are large, round and very neat.

Tail: Of good length, thick at the base and showing only a very modest tapering to the rounded tip.

This beautiful Bengal shows the striking, lime-green eyes characteristic of the breed. Photo by Isabelle Francais.

Coat: Short, silky and dense, it exhibits a plush sheen.

Color: There are three colors at this time: leopard, golden and snow. The leopard has black spots on a rufus ground color. The golden has dark to reddish spots on a golden ground. The snow leopard has dark spots on a silver ground. In each color, the whisker pads, chin and chest are white. The spots are scattered at random or in horizontal lines along the body. The tail and legs are barred with broken bracelets. The head carries tabby markings and pencil lines from the eye and cheek on each side of the face.

Bad Faults: Kink in tail, spots which coalesce on the body.

Remarks: The Bengal is a very impressive-looking cat. Like all spotted breeds, it is currently very much in vogue. Its Asiatic wild ancestor is one of the most agile of all felines and displays a strong liking for water, which it enters on a regular basis. The cost of the breed may inhibit its purchase. If you do acquire a kitten, be very sure you keep an eye on it; sadly, it is a prime target for cat thieves. This comment applies to any of the spotted breeds, which always look so impressive.

BENGAL, LEOPARD
Female

BIRMAN

HISTORY: The true origins of the Birman are unknown, but the breed is associated with the temples of Burma, thus its alternative name of the Sacred Cat of Burma. This was applied to it by the French, who are credited with the breed's development, and who prepared the original breed standard adopted by all other nations. The Birman can be viewed in two ways, that of the legend that surrounds its color creation, and the actual genetic base to the breed.

The legend states that in the temple of Lao-Tsun there were many pure white cats, which were the reincarnation of former priests. The temple housed Tsun-Kyan-Kse, a golden goddess with sapphire blue eyes. She watched over the migration of the souls from the priests to the cats. One night a temple priest, Mun-Ha, was praying in front of the goddess. Beside him was the cat Sinh, his constant companion. The temple was attacked and the priest was killed. At the moment of the priest's death, Sinh stood on his body and turned to face the goddess. The white fur turned golden brown, becoming darker at the cat's bodily extremities. Sinh's eyes became a beautiful blue, but the white of the paws remained unchanged — a sign of the cat's purity of spirit. By the following morning all of the temple cats had acquired the same colors as Sinh.

At a later date the priests were forced to leave their temple and move to Tibet. They were aided in this by many Europeans, including French and Englishmen. It is said a pair of temple cats were sent to France as a token of the priests' appreciation, this being in 1919. Thereafter, the breed steadily grew in popularity and was improved, both in France and Germany. The breed was recognized in France in 1925. It gained championship status in the UK in 1966, and in the USA in 1967. Since the 1960s the breed has increased its numbers steadily each year. The Birman is an unlikely Asian cat. Its conformation strongly suggests that in its development it has been crossed with European longhaired stock, possibly of Persian origin. The basic color pattern is that of a Siamese, with the white feet being the result of what is termed dominant white spotting. Genetically, it is thus a mixed bag. The result, however, is an extremely attractive feline.

ALLOWABLE OUTCROSSES: None.

RECOGNITION: All associations.

DESCRIPTION

Head: Broad and round. Cheeks well developed as is the chin. The nose is described as medium in length. The CFA standard calls for a

BIRMAN, CHOCOLATE POINT
Male

BIRMAN, BLUE POINT
Male, Kitten

BIRMAN, LILAC POINT
Female

BIRMAN, SEAL POINT
Male, Double Grand Champion

slightly Roman (convex) nose.

Ears: Medium in size, spaced well apart, and terminating in a rounded tip.

Eyes: Almost round in shape and set well apart. There is a very slight upward incline, but not in any way comparable to that of the Siamese type breeds. The color is blue — the deeper the better.

Body: Long and massive. Well muscled.

Legs & Feet: Of medium length and thick. Paws short, large and round, as befits a powerfully built cat.

Tail: Medium in length and in a pleasing proportion to the body length.

Coat: Medium to long, and silky in texture. There is a full ruff around the neck and the hair on the stomach is slightly curled. The fur's silk texture reduces the matting potential.

Color: In the USA only the original Siamese colors are accepted. These are as follows:

Seal Point: body is pale fawn to cream, becoming a lighter hue on the stomach and chest. Points seal brown. Shading on back and sides to compliment the points.

Blue Point: body bluish white to pale ivory, becoming almost white on stomach and chest. Points deep blue. Shading on back and sides to compliment the points.

Chocolate Point: body ivory. Points milk chocolate. No shading.

Lilac Point: body almost white (magnolia). Points frost gray with a pinkish hue. No shading.

In Great Britain only the Seal and Blue points presently have full status. However, the following colors have preliminary recognition and will in due course gain full status.

Chocolate Point: as above. Shading to tone with points.

Lilac Point: as above. Shading to tone with points.

Red Point: body pale cream with golden hue. Points orange-red.

Seal Tortie Point: body color fawn, shading unevenly to brown/pale red on back and sides. Points seal brown intermingled with light and dark red.

Cream Point: body off white with a golden hue. Points cream.

BIRMAN, SEAL POINT
Male, Single Grand Champion
Nine months old

Blue Tortie Point: body off white shading to pale blue-cream. Points blue intermingled with cream.

Chocolate Tortie Point: body ivory shading to pale chocolate—red. Points chocolate intermingled with light and dark red.

Lilac Tortie Point: body off white shading to pale lilac-cream.

Points: lilac intermingled with cream.

Seal Tabby Point: body pale beige with golden hue, preferably free of shading. If present the latter should be the point color. Points: Seal tabby. 'M' marking on forehead, eye markings. Ears free of stripes. Tail ringed. Legs should carry distinct rings or stripes above the gauntlets.

Blue Tabby Point: body color bluish white, preferably without shading. Points blue tabby with markings as for seal tabby point.

Feet: These are an important characteristic of the Birman. The white paws are called gloves, the rear are often called gauntlets. Those of the front should be symmetrical and pure white. They should not extend beyond the ankle. The rear gloves should cover the entire paw and taper up the back of the feet to end below the hock. The tapering part is called the lace. In the ideal cat the gloves of the front feet match, as do those and the laces of the rear feet. However, this state is extremely rare. It is a matter of pure chance just how well matched the gloves are.

Bad Faults: Poor bone structure, a kink in the tail, missing white on any paw, a color in the gloves, any tendency towards Siamese type, white on laces extending beyond the hock, a squint in one or both eyes. A squint is when the eye appears to be looking at the nose.

Remarks: The Birman is a breed with a very interesting background. It combines good looks with a long coat that is not prone to heavy tangling. However, grooming at least every other day is recommended. It is not easy to breed quality Birmans of a good show standard because of the 'pot luck' aspect of the gloves.

BOMBAY

HISTORY: The Bombay is a breed that was planned, not a chance happening. The two original cats that founded the breed were both Grand Champions: one was a black American Shorthair and the other was a sable Burmese. Any pairing of these two breeds, plus Bombay-to-Bombay, is thus a representative of this very attractive breed. The name is derived from the fact that the breed is thought to resemble the black panther, which is the melanistic (black) variety of the leopard. The latter is native to both Africa and Asia. There is thus no direct link of the name to the city in India. In the UK the Bombay is a member of the GCCF group of Asian breeds, which are those of Burmese type in non-Burmese colors.

ALLOWABLE OUTCROSSES: Black American Shorthair (USA): black British Shorthair (UK): Sable Burmese.

RECOGNITION: American Associations,GCCF.

DESCRIPTION

Head: Pleasingly rounded with no sharp angles. Good breadth between the eyes. Short well-developed muzzle. In profile an obvious nose break should be apparent. This should not in any way be snubbed. It should be a curve. When viewed from the front the skull has a slight dome.

Ears: Medium in size, they are set well apart. They are broad at the base, tapering to a rounded tip. They are inclined just slightly forward when viewed in profile.

Eyes: Set far apart, round and with a rounded aperture. The color is gold to copper, the more deep and brilliant the better.

Body: Medium in size, never cobby or svelte in appearance, the Bombay is muscular and surprisingly heavy for its looks. The back line is level from shoulders to tail. The shoulders and rump are of the same width.

Legs & Feet: Neither long nor short, they should be proportionate to the body. The feet are round, muscular and compact.

Tail: Medium in length, neither thick nor whip-like, the tip should be nicely rounded.

Coat: Short, fine and laying close to the body. It should give the appearance of shimmering patent leather, a characteristic of this breed. Very silky to the touch.

Color: Dense coal black to the roots. However, kittens may take time to develop the full

black pigmentation and the patent gloss to the fur.

Bad Faults: Cobbiness or ranginess, green-colored eyes, kink in the tail, lack of sheen to the coat, lack of black hair to the roots, any other color seen in the coat. An excessive nose break.

Remarks: The Bombay represents the balance between the extremes of the black American or British Shorthairs on the one hand and the rangy svelte bodies of the Oriental Shorthairs on the other. The temperament of the breed can also vary from the somewhat more staid of the shorthairs to the more outgoing nature common to most cats of foreign type.

BOMBAY
Male

BOMBAY
Female
Six months old

Bombay
Male, Champion
Twenty-five months old

BRITISH SHORTHAIR

HISTORY: The British Shorthair has a history that broadly parallels the American Shorthair. The British cat is the ancestor of its American cousin and has, of course, been around for a few centuries longer. It is the farm and street cat of Britain, thought to have been introduced to that country by the Romans. When the first cat show was staged in London, there were a number of British Shorthairs. As the years rolled by, the registered cats fell into decline due to the competition from Persians, Siamese and other exotics.

World War II devastated the purebred British stock, and after the war ended some of the remaining stock was bred to Persians. This was frowned on by the GCCF and quickly stopped once the gene pool of the British Shorthair was considered sound. By the 1950s, the breed was once again becoming popular in shows — a trend that has continued to this day with the breed now ranked fourth in its homeland in terms of registered numbers in 1990. The blue, the silver tabby, and the spotted have especially gained an international reputation for their excellence. The breed's popularity in the USA has been very steady, in spite of the obvious competition from its American cousin.

ALLOWABLE OUTCROSSES: None.

RECOGNITION: All associations.

DESCRIPTION

Head: Round with full cheeks and set on a short thick neck.

Ears: Small and rounded at the tips. Set far apart and fitting into the rounded contour of the skull.

Eyes: Large and round, set well apart and with no tendency towards oriental or a squint (when one or both eyes looks towards the nose).

Body: Cobby, with a sort level back. Low on the leg, and with a broad chest. Massive across the shoulders and rump as befits a cat with a hardy background. Medium to large in size - but never rangy.

Legs & Feet: Relatively short in comparison to the bulk of the body, the legs are of good bone and muscle to carry the weight. Feet round and firm.

Tail: Medium in length it is thick at the base and slowly tapers to a rounded tip.

Coat: Short, dense. Firm to the touch. It should never be overlong or woolly. Some are of a more silky texture and look than others, though the standards are the same for all color varieties in terms of texture.

Color: The British Shorthair is available in just about every color and pattern known to exist in cats. In Britain, all of these colors and patterns are accepted. In other countires, the various associations may only recognize certain of them at this time. The major ones are as follows:

SELF COLORS

White: Pure and untinged with yellow. The eye color is either deep sapphire blue, copper through orange to deep gold, or odd-eyed, which means one eye in blue and one in copper-gold. Paw pads and nose leather are pink.

Black: Jet black to the roots. No rusty tinge or white hairs. Eye color is copper, orange or deep gold. Paw pads and nose leather are black.

Blue: Light to medium blue (the lighter shades preferred in the USA). The color should be even throughout the coat, with no tabby markings, white or silver tipping. Eye color is copper, orange or deep gold. Paw pads and nose leather are blue.

Chocolate: Any shade of rich dark brown. No markings, white or shading of any kind. Eye color is copper, orange or gold, with no trace of green. Paw pads pinkish, nose leather to match the coat color.

Lilac: A frosty gray with a pinkish tone. No tabby markings to be evident in adults. Eye color copper, orange or gold. Paw pads and nose leather pinkish.

Red: Deep rich red with as few tabby markings as possible. No white hairs anywhere. Eye color copper or orange with no trace of green. Paw pads and nose leather brick red.

BRITISH SHORTHAIR, BLACK AND WHITE
Male

BRITISH SHORTHAIR, WHITE
Male
One year and ten months old

Cream: This is a dilute red so is neither red nor fawn but a pale cream. As free of tabby markings as possible. No white hairs anywhere. Eye color is copper, orange or deep gold. Paw pads and nose leather are pink.

TABBY PATTERN

You can select from any of three tabby patterns — classic, mackerel or spotted. These are seen in the following colors:

Brown: Ground color is a rich copper brown on which the tabby pattern is superimposed in dense black. Eye color copper, orange or gold. Paw pads black, nose leather brick red or black.

Silver: Ground color is silver, tabby pattern is dense black. Eye color green or hazel. Paw pads black, nose leather brick red or black.

Blue: Ground color is a bluish fawn, tabby pattern a dark blue. Eye color is copper, orange or gold with no trace of green. Paw pads and nose leather are blue or pink.

Red: Ground color red, tabby pattern dark rich red showing good contrast against ground color. Eye color deep orange or copper. Paw pads and nose leather are red.

Cream: Ground color is a very pale cream, tabby pattern a buff or dark cream, to show contrast against ground color. Eye color is copper or gold. Paw pads and nose leather are pink.

TORTOISESHELL

A mixture of black, rich red and pale red evenly intermingled over the whole body, without any obvious patches of any color. Eye color is deep orange or copper. Paw pads and nose leather are pink and/or black.

Blue-Cream: A mixture of medium blue and pale cream intermingled as in the tortoiseshell. Eye color is copper, orange or deep gold. Paw pads and nose leather are pink and/or blue.

Chocolate Tortie: As for the tortoiseshell. The black is replaced by chocolate. Eye color is copper, orange or gold with no trace of green.

Paw pads and nose leather are chocolate.

Tortoiseshell and White (Calico in USA): Patches of black, red and white. At least one third and not more than one half of the coat to be white. The blue tortie and white is the same as the tortie and white; the black is replaced with blue, and the red by pale cream. Eye color is copper, deep orange, or gold. Paw pads and nose leather are black and/or pink, or blue and/or pink, as applicable to the body color.

BICOLORS

The bicolor coat contains self color patches and white, the latter to occupy at least one third, but no more than half, of the coat. A white blaze is desirable in the USA. Any self color and white is acceptable. Eye color is copper, orange or deep gold. Paw pads and nose leather will be the color of the coat and/or pink.

POINTED (HIMALAYAN) PATTERN

The mask, ears, legs and tail should be a clearly defined color, matching on all points. The body color will be lighter. If shading is seen, this should tone with that of the points. All of the self colors, as well as tortie point, tabby point, and tortie tabby point, are available in British Shorthairs. In all pointed colors and patterns the eye color is blue. The paw pads and nose leathers will be as appropriate to the body color.

SMOKES AND TIPPED PATTERNS

In both the smoke and the tipped patterns the underfur is a silvery white. In the smokes, the color extends well down the hair shaft. In the tipped, it is restricted to the very ends of the hair, thus creating a very subtle shading. All recognized colors and patterns are acceptable. The eye color in the smokes is copper, orange, or deep gold. These colors also apply to the tipped colors, with the exception of black-tipped coats, in which case the eye color is green. The paw pads and nose leather color will be as appropriate to the colors of the coat tipping.

BRITISH SHORTHAIR, BLUE
Male

Bad Faults: Jaw and mouth deformities, overlong, soft or fluffy coats, pronounced whisker pads, kinks in tail, incorrect eye color, white on any color in which this is not required.

Remarks: The British Shorthair is a very hardy cat with a quiet nature. Its coat is undemanding, and it makes a super pet or exhibition animal. The tabbies and spotted pattern are quite outstanding in this breed.

BRITISH SHORTHAIR, BLUE
Female, Grand Champion

BRITISH SHORTHAIR, BLACK
Male
Eight months old

BURMESE

HISTORY: Although the origins of the Burmese are common to the USA and Great Britain, you might not think so if you saw examples from each country. The breed was developed from a program that commenced with a brown cat imported from Burma into the USA by Joseph Thompson in 1930. This female cat, Wong Mau, was paired to a good Siamese, and the beginnings of the Burmese were put in motion. It took many years to stabilize the breed using Siamese and imported foreign stock. The Burmese was initially recognized in the USA in 1936. This status was withdrawn in 1947. It was not reinstated until 1957, five years after the British had recognized the breed. Although the standards of the USA and the UK are broadly similar, the British prefer a somewhat Oriental-looking cat, whereas in the USA a more solid stocky cat is the favored choice.

ALLOWABLE OUTCROSSES: None.

RECOGNITION: All associations.

DESCRIPTION

Head: When viewed from the front the head is round, with a slight dome to the skull. In the UK a modified wedge is preferred but without being of the Siamese type. There should be plenty of breadth between the ears. If you view many Burmese, you will notice there is quite some variation in the shape of the head, not withstanding the requirements of the standard.

Ears: Medium in size, broad at their base and tapering to a rounded tip.

Eyes: Large and with rounded aperture (CFA). Large and with the top line of the eye showing a straight Oriental slant towards the nose, the lower line being rounded (GCCF). The color is yellow to gold (CFA), and any shade of yellow from chartreuse to amber, with golden yellow preferred (GCCF). Green eyes are a serious fault in this breed.

BURMESE, SABLE
Female, Kitten
Four months old

BURMESE, CHAMPAGNE
Male

BURMESE, CHAMPAGNE
Female, Champion

BURMESE, SABLE
Male, Grand Champion

Body: Medium in size, but heavy. The back line is level, the chest round, and the whole package presents a muscular appearance.

Legs & Feet: The CFA standard simply states well proportioned to the body, whereas that of the GCCF adds they should be slender, the hind legs slightly longer than the front. Paws are round (CFA) or oval (GCCF).

Tail: Straight, medium in length, is the CFA requirement. The GCCF requires the same but adds not heavy at the base, and tapering only slightly to a rounded tip, without bone defect.

Coat: This must be short, fine, glossy, and satin-like in texture, lying close to the body.

Some of the newer colors now seen in the breed include the following: red, cream, brown tortie, blue tortie (blue-cream, chocolate tortie, and lilac tortie.

In the last four colors the paw pads and nose leather will be either plain or blotched with the color and pink. In the red and cream colors these will be pink. In the four tortie colors markings will be seen in the coat. Extra marks are given for the type in lieu of color quality.

BURMESE, CREAM
Male
One year old

Color: The colors seen in the Burmese will reflect the association in question. The GCCF accepts many colors but American registries stick with the original four colors of sable (brown in UK), champagne (chocolate in UK), blue, and platinum (Lilac in UK). In each color this should shade almost imperceptibly to a slightly lighter shade on the underparts. Other than this, and slightly darker ears and mask, there should be no marks or barrings at all. In actual fact the tail will also tend to be rather darker in color and will invariably match the mask. The paw pads and nose leather will reflect the body color.

Bad Faults: Kink in tail, incorrect eye color, white buttons or lockets, cobbyness, and any tendency towards the extremes of shape seen in the Siamese.

Remarks: The Burmese is a truly delightful breed that should satisfy the most discerning of owners. It displays the obvious curiosity and intelligence to things around it that is a trait of the Oriental breeds. Although regarded as an American breed, it is more popular in Great Britain, where only the Persian and the Siamese outnumber it in annual registrations.

BURMESE, CHOCOLATE
Female, Champion
One year old

BURMESE, SABLE
Female

BURMESE, CHAMPAGNE
Female

BURMESE, SABLE
Male, Kitten
Six months old

CHARTREUX

HISTORY: The Chartreux is a very old breed of France that is thought to have existed for a number of centuries. However, it was not until the late 1920s that breeders decided to develop the Chartreux. It was first exhibited under its breed name in 1931 in Paris. During World War II the breed's numbers were all but decimated, so in reconstructing the Chartreux, British Blues in particular were used to try to correct matters. However, this was not entirely satisfactory, so local cats that met the requirements were used to form a base foundation stock. From this, and what was available of the breed, the present cat has resulted.

ALLOWABLE OUTCROSSES: None.

RECOGNITION: All American associations.

DESCRIPTION

Head: Rounded, but with well developed cheeks that give the breed a wide-faced look. The nose is of medium length and quite wide. There is a slight nose break at the forehead, which should be a very gentle curve.The neck is short and thick.

Ears: Medium in height and width. Very erect posture, and just rounded at their tips.

Eyes: Although described as round they often appear more almond in shape and with a very slight slant towards the ears.

Body: A large cat with a powerful frame and plenty of substance. Broad shoulders and wide chest.

Legs & Feet: Medium in length and muscular, giving the impression of larger bone size than is actually the case. Paws round.

Tail: Moderate in length, thick at base and tapering to an oval tip.

Coat: Medium in length, dense and slightly woolly to the touch. The degree of woolliness is dependent on the sex of the cat, its age, and the habitat (temperature) it lives in.

Color: You can choose from any color as long as it's blue! The shade is blue gray from ash to slate. Hairs tips ever so slightly brushed with silver. The emphasis is on uniformity and clarity rather than shade, though the preferred tone is light. The paw pads are rose-taupe and the nose leather is slate gray.

Bad Faults: Lack of substance, severe nose break, snub nose, eyes too close together, and any white lockets in the coat.

Remarks: The Chartreux is a very desirable breed, having many virtues and no vices. However, it remains a rare breed whose numbers have barely risen over the last decade. This is possibly because the competition, in the form of the British and Russian Blues, is more well known, and thus better established.

This mature Chartreux clearly has the powerful build typical of the breed. Photo by Isabelle Francais.

CHARTREUX, BLUE
Female, Kitten

CORNISH REX

HISTORY: As mutations go, that which produces the rex coat is one of the most numerous. However, when it appeared in a litter born to farm cats near Bodmin, Cornwall, it caused quite a sensation. That first rex was named Kallibunker, who was thus the founder of the breed called the English Rex, later renamed the Cornish Rex. The mutation not only changed the coat of the cat, but also its appearance, for it looked nothing like its domestic shorthair parents — a tortie and white (calico) female and a ginger tabby male. The owner of this rex, Mrs Ennismore, sought the counsel of the well-known cat authority, Stirling-Webb. A new breed was underway.

The Cornish Rex gained recognition in the UK in 1967. It had to wait for some years before it was accorded full status in the USA. It was first imported into the States in 1957 via a female mated to Poldu, the first son of Kallibunker. The breed has proved more popular in the USA than the Devon Rex, which is a reverse of the situation in its homeland. That the Cornish Rex is an independent breed to the Devon Rex can easily be proven. When a Cornish is mated to a Devon all of the resulting kittens will have normal fur, thus establishing the fact that the genes creating the rex mutations are at differing loci in the respective breeds.

CORNISH REX, CALICO
Female

ALLOWABLE OUTCROSSES: None.

RECOGNITION: All associations.

DESCRIPTION

Head: A medium wedge, the length of the head is about one third longer than its maximum width. When viewed from the front there is a definite whisker break — the area just behind the points where the whiskers are located.

Ears: Large and set high on the head. Wide at the base, they taper to a gently rounded tip.

Eyes: Medium in size, they are oval in shape and have a very slight Oriental slant. There should be a full eye's width between them across the bridge of the nose. The color should be appropriate to the coat color, or green through yellow. The latter does not apply to the Si-Rex (a Siamese-patterned rex).

Body: Small to medium. Torso longish. The back is naturally arched, this being evident when the cat stands in a natural position.

Legs & Feet: Long and slender, giving the impression that the cat is high on the leg. The legs should be straight. Small and oval.

Tail: Long, slender, and tapering to a rounded tip.

Coat: The coat is, of course, the main characteristic of this breed. It is short, plush, silky and relatively dense. While there is not an absence of guard hairs, these are minimal. The UK standard (GCCF) states 'without guard hairs.' The fur on the head, back, sides, and tail forms ripples, or marcel waves. The whiskers are crinkled and bent.

Color: All coat colors and patterns are acceptable. Asymmetrical white markings are allowed in this breed. White markings are not allowed on cats with the Siamese pattern (Si-Rex).

Bad Faults: Sparse coats and those displaying bare patches. Shaggy, or too short a coat. Small ears, cobby body, short tail, and kinks in tail.

CORNISH REX, TORTOISESHELL AND WHITE
Female, Novice
Four months old

Remarks: The Cornish Rex is not a breed that will appeal to everyone because its coat is quite distinctive. You will either love it or feel it just doesn't look right. An individual with a full dense coat is very impressive. Those with poor coats are the ones not likely to appeal. There are no adverse side effects to the coat mutation. This so, the only extra consideration any rex breed owner should bear in mind is that the coat does not provide the full protection of a regular cat's coat, so it will appreciate a nice warm room on those cold and wet days.

CORNISH REX, BLUE
Male, Single Grand Champion
Three years and three months old

CORNISH REX, BLACK AND WHITE BICOLOR
Female, Kitten

CORNISH REX, BLACK SMOKE AND WHITE
BICOLOR
Male, Grand Champion

CORNISH REX, RED MACKEREL TABBY
Neutered male, Novice
Two years and seven months old

THE WORLD'S LARGEST SELECTION OF PET AND ANIMAL BOOKS
T.F.H. Publications publishes more than 900 books covering many hobby aspects (dogs,

. . **CATS** . . .

. . . **BIRDS** . .

. . . **ANIMALS** . . .

. . . **DOGS** . .

. . **FISH** . . .

cats, birds, fish, small animals, etc.), plus books dealing with more purely scientific aspects of the animal world (such as books about fossils, corals, sea shells, whales and octopuses). Whether you are a beginner or an advanced hobbyist you will find exactly what you're looking for among our complete listing of books. For a free catalog fill out the form on the other side of this page and mail it today. All T.F.H. books are recyclable.

CORNISH REX, TORTOISESHELL AND WHITE
Female, Kitten

CORNISH REX, BROWN MACKEREL TABBY
AND WHITE
Male

CORNISH REX, TORTOISESHELL
Female, Double Grand Champion

CORNISH REX, TORTIE POINT
Female, Kitten

CORNISH REX, RED MACKEREL TABBY
Male, Kitten

CORNISH REX, RED MACKEREL TABBY AND
WHITE
Female, Kitten

CYMRIC

HISTORY: The Cymric, although it sports a Welsh sounding name, has it origins in Canada. It is a longhaired Manx, the mutation appearing in the 1960s. The standard for the Cymric, and the available colors, is exactly the same as that for the Manx. You are therefore referred to that breed for all details other than that of the coat, which is described here.

ALLOWABLE OUTCROSSES: Manx.

RECOGNITION: Fully recognized in some, pro visional in other registries.

DESCRIPTION

Coat: Medium length and dense. The fur on the ruff of the neck, the breeches, and the abdomen are of longer length than on the body. The cheek fur is thick. The neck ruff extends to form a bib on the chest. Toe and ear tufts of hair are desirable. The texture of the coat is soft and silky. It lays flat but full due to its double nature — all three hair types being present. The breed is slow to mature, so young Cymrics will not display the coat of the adult.

Remarks: The Cymric is an attractive breed that will attract a limited number of followers. However, the physical problems that are associated with its parent breed must be considered by would-be owners.

CYMRIC, TORTOISESHELL
Female

CYMRIC, BROWN CLASSIC TABBY
Male

CYMRIC, RED MACKEREL TABBY
Male, Champion

DEVON REX

HISTORY: The second of the rex breeds, the Devon, appeared in a litter of domestic shorthaired British cats in 1960, ten years after the Cornish Rex. Ironically, the event happened in the county next to Cornwall, in the home of Beryl Cox of Buckfastleigh. The kitten, a black-haired male called Kirlee, was purchased by Brien Stirling-Webb, who had some involvement in the development of the Cornish Rex. No doubt he was surprised when a mating to his Cornish Rex resulted in 100% normal-haired kittens. He quickly appreciated that the only answer to this apparently unexpected result was that while the two rex mutations were simple recessives, the genes that controlled them were at separate loci. A new breed was thus created. After the arrival of the Cornish Rex, others appeared in 1951 (Italy and East Germany), 1952 (Ohio), 1959 (Oregon), and California (1960). However, only the Cornish and Devon Rexes have gained international recognition.

ALLOWABLE OUTCROSSES: None.

RECOGNITION: All associations.

DESCRIPTION

Head: Often described as pixie or elf-like, the head of the Devon Rex forms a modified wedge when viewed from the front. The cheeks are full, much more so than in the Cornish Rex. There is a whisker break and the muzzle is short. The nose has a distinct break or stop and the forehead curves back to a flat skull.

DEVON REX, BROWN MACKEREL TABBY
Male, Kitten

Ears: Large and set low into the head. Wide at the base, they taper to a rounded tip. The angles of the ears are such that they complement the width of the head when compared to the Cornish Rex.

Eyes: Oval in shape, they are large and wide set, with a slight slope in the direction of the ear tips. Color should be appropriate to the coat color or, except in the Si-Rex, chartreuse, green or yellow.

Body: Of medium length, the body should be muscular. The chest is broad and seemingly carried high on the legs.

Legs & Feet: Tall and slender, with the hind legs longer than those of the front. The paws are small and oval.

Tail: Long, fine and tapering, well covered with short fur.

DEVON REX, WHITE
Female, Kitten

Coat: Very short, the coat has a rippled effect. It is soft, wavy or curly. The fur is dense on the back, sides, tail, and legs. It is less dense on the head, chest, and abdomen — but should not be missing, which is a serious fault in an adult. The whiskers are bent or crimped and tend to break so there is rarely a full complement. The Devon suffers rather more than the Cornish in terms of loss of hair.

Color: All colors and coat patterns are accepted in the Devon Rex, but white markings in the coat of a Si-Rex would earn disqualification in a show animal. The Si-Rex is not a separate variety, but a cat displaying the Siamese coat pattern.

Remarks: Although the coats of the Devon and Cornish Rexes are slightly different, the main distinguishing feature on which you would likely choose one or the other will be in the shape and features of the face. As in any breed that is seen in almost all colors and patterns, do remember that the facial colors can considerably alter the apparent expression on a cat's face. This is because the color can highlight differing facial aspects or, in the case of self colors, give equal, thus balanced, expression.

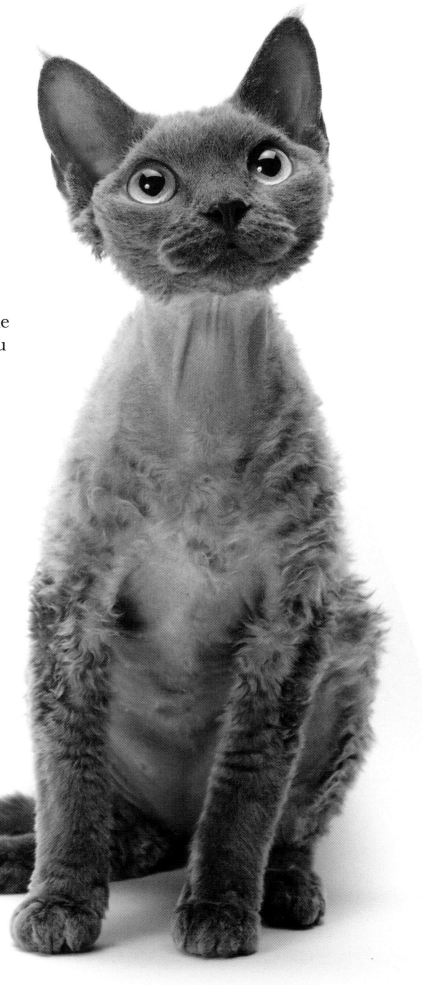

DEVON REX, BLUE
Female

DEVON REX, BROWN MACKEREL TABBY
Male, Double Grand Champion

DEVON REX, WHITE
Female

DEVON REX, WHITE
Male, Kitten

DEVON REX, BLACK
Female

EGYPTIAN MAU

HISTORY: Spotted cats, in a domestic situation, have appeared in paintings and artifacts dating back over one thousand years. It is therefore natural that owners of the Egyptian like to believe that this breed has some direct connection with the sacred cats of Egypt. This is true to the degree that the founder cats of the breed came from Cairo and were spotted — beyond that nothing is known. The first of this breed to be seen in the USA were imported from Rome, where they had been exhibited about 1954. They were first shown in the USA in1957 and gained championship status with the CFF in 1968. The CFA accorded them status in 1979. They are not recognized in the UK, where they are regarded as being of Siamese origin and classified as Oriental Shorthairs of the tabby group.

ALLOWABLE OUTCROSSES: None.

RECOGNITION: All American associations.

DESCRIPTION

Head: Of an oriental wedge shape, there is a definite whisker break. The muzzle is of medium length, the nose straight along its entire length. The skull between the ears has a very gentle curve, being neither domed nor flat. The neck is strong and of a good length.

Ears: Medium to large, their base is wide. They taper to a rounded tip. The line of the outer edge of the ear continues in a straight line into the cheeks when viewed from the front.

Eyes: Large and almond in shape, they exhibit a very slight slant towards the ears. Their color is a light gooseberry green, though an

EGYPTIAN MAU, BLACK SMOKE
Male

EGYPTIAN MAU, SILVER
Female

amber cast is permissible in young cats up to the age of 18 months of age.

Body: Moderate in length, the Egyptian should be muscular without be overly broad.

Legs & Feet: Long and slim, the hind legs are longer than the front. The paws are oval and compact, never hare-like.

Tail: Medium in length, it exhibits a steady taper to its tip.

Coat: Fine and silky to the touch, it must display a good sheen. The length is short but long enough to accommodate at least two bars of ticking.

GENERAL COAT PATTERN (APPLICABLE TO ALL COLORS)

Forehead barred with tabby 'M' mark. Cheeks barred with two 'mascara' lines, one from the eye and one from the cheeks. The upper chest contains one or more broken necklaces, while similar broken bars are found on the legs and haunches. The spots on the body vary in size and should be well formed. They need not match on either side of the body.

Color: Originally there were just three color patterns. However, two additional colors, pewter and black, are now gaining acceptance.

Silver: A pale silver ground, which becomes lighter on the underparts. The spots and other markings are a charcoal black color over a white to silver hair-base. They should show good contrast against the ground color. Nose, lips and eyes outlined in black. The upper throat, chin and nostril areas are very pale, appearing almost white. Paw pads black. Nose leather brick red.

Bronze: A light brown ground color on which the dark brown to black marks, over a light brown hair base, are superimposed. Nose, lines and eyes outlined in brown. Upper throat, chin and nostrils a creamy white. Paw pads black or dark brown. Nose leather brick red.

Smoke: A pale silver ground. Spots and markings jet black over a white to silver hair base. Nose, lips and eyes outlined in jet black. The upper throat, chin and nostril areas are the lightest shade of the ground color. Paw pads and nose leather are black.

Pewter: A light rose-gray ground color with brown markings. Paw pads brown. Nose leather brick red.

Black: The same as the smoke, but the hairs of the spots and markings are to be black to the roots.

larity. The would-be owner should seek out good examples of the breed because some can look rather too oriental when compared with the cats originally imported as members of this breed.

EGYPTIAN MAU, SILVER
Female, Kitten

Bad Faults: Body too cobby or too lithe. Lack of spots or coalescence of body spots into stripes. Blue eyes. Kink in tail. White buttons or lockets. Remarks: The Egyptian Mau (*Mau* simply meaning cat) is one of a number of spotted cats that are presently gaining in popu-

EGYPTIAN MAU, BRONZE
Male

EXOTIC SHORTHAIR

HISTORY: The origins of this breed can be traced back to the period that commenced in the early 1950s. In Great Britain, Persians were crossed with British Shorthairs in order to gain type that had been lost as a result of the devastation caused during World War II. This was quickly stopped, as many breeders objected to the practice. In the USA the reason was different. Breeders in American Shorthairs found that their cats were not winning major awards — the Persian sweeping all before it.

In order to make the American Shorthair more glamorous, exhibitors started to cross their cats with Persians so they would create a 'new look' to the face and fur of the American Shorthair. This also caused much controversy, so a new class for these hybrids came into being during 1966. A standard was set; this was for the Persian type but with relatively short hair. Any cat that more closely resembled the Exotic Shorthair than an American Shorthair was allowed to change over to be part of the new breed. Although the original outcrosses included the Burmese, this breed was eventually dropped so that only the Persian and the American Shorthair were accepted crosses. The breed

proved very popular and has now also gained preliminary recognition in Great Britain. The Exotic Shorthair is thus a Persian in all aspects other than coat length.

ALLOWABLE OUTCROSSES: Persian only.

RECOGNITION: All associations.

DESCRIPTION

Head: Round and massive with full cheeks that make the face wider than it is tall, the ratio being approximately as five is to four. The neck is short and thick. The nose is short, snub, and with an obvious break at the forehead. As with

EXOTIC SHORTHAIR, BLUE AND WHITE
Female

the Persian, the facial expression in this breed is quite variable, depending on the length of the nose.

Ears: Set low in the head, they are relatively small and not unduly open at their base. They taper to a small rounded tip.

Eyes: Large and round, they are set far apart. Their color will depend on the coat color.

Body: Cobby in type, broad and deep of the chest, massive across both the shoulders and the rump. The appearance must be of a substantial cat that is set low on the leg. Size is medium to large but overall proportions more important than sheer size.

Legs & Feet: Short, thick and muscular. The front legs should be straight. The paws are large, round and firm.

Tail: On the short side. It should look in harmonious balance to the overall body.

Coat: Dense, plush and soft in texture. It is longer than in many shorthairs but not so long that it flows. Its density causes it to stand a little out from the body, though still laying flattish.

EXOTIC SHORTHAIR, BLUE
Male, Grand Champion

EXOTIC SHORTHAIR, BLUE
Male, Champion

EXOTIC SHORTHAIR, BLACK AND WHITE
Female, Kitten

EXOTIC SHORTHAIR, BLACK AND WHITE
Male, Grand Champion

EXOTIC SHORTHAIR, BLACK
Female, Grand Champion

Color: The Exotic is seen in all the colors and patterns exhibited by both the Persian and the American or British Shorthairs. This means in just about every color and pattern seen in cats. This so, you are referred to the breeds named for color descriptions.

Bad Faults: Kink in tail, abnormality of the jaws, white lockets or buttons on a colored part of the coat, incorrect eye color, lack of substance, and any apparent weakness of the limbs.

Remarks: The Exotic Shorthair has all of the attributes of its parent breeds. The pleasing looks of a Persian and the plush, yet very manageable coat of a shorthair, combine to produce a cat that enjoys growing popularity in the USA and is rapidly climbing the chart in the UK and elsewhere.

HAVANA (BROWN)

HISTORY: The Havana was a planned breed created in England during the 1950s. The original recipe was a sealpoint Siamese crossed to a self-black shorthair. In fact, a number of pairings were used. These included Siamese x Russian blue. Eventually, the chestnut brown Havana was established but was named the Chestnut Brown Foreign Shorthair. This was changed in 1971 to its present name. In Britain, a cat of foreign type is desired, the breed being classed as an Oriental Shorthair. In the USA, after importing original British stock, the foreign type was bred out by never mating back to a Siamese. The result is that the Havana breed of England more closely resembles the chestnut Oriental Shorthair of the USA. The American Havana Brown is a less svelte and oriental-looking cat.

ALLOWABLE OUTCROSSES: None.

RECOGNITION: All associations.

DESCRIPTION

Head: A triangle is formed when viewed from the front. The sides of it are formed by straight lines from the ears to the nose. In the USA a more rounded face is the desired shape, as is a whisker break, which is not required in the UK. In profile the head is wedge shaped — neither round nor pointed. There is no stop or nose break in the UK Havana but a definite one in the Havana Brown of the USA.

Ears: Large and tapering to a rounded point, their outer edge forms part of the line of the wedge.

Eyes: Oriental in shape and slanting towards

HAVANA, CHOCOLATE
Male, Champion

HAVANA, CHOCOLATE
Female

HAVANA, FROST
Female

the nose (GCCF). Oval in shape; set wide apart (CFA). The color is clear, bright vivid green (UK), the deeper the green the better (USA).

Body: Medium in size, long and svelte (GCCF), medium in length, firm and muscular (CFA). In the USA a body midway between short coupled and svelte is the desired type.

Legs & Feet: Long and thin, the back legs are taller than the front. The paws are small and oval.

Tail: Long and tapering — but not blunt ended. Should not be too thick at the base.

Coat: Very short and silky in texture, it should lie close to the body. In the USA the coat is required to be short to medium in length.

Color: Rich warm chestnut brown. Not dark or cold toned (GCCF). A rich and even shade of warm brown throughout; color tends toward red-brown (mahogany) rather than black-brown (CFA). Paw pads and nose leather are solid brown or solid pinkish brown. In the UK the dilution of the Havana color is the lilac, which is called the Foreign lilac and judged, like the Havana, to the standard of Oriental Shorthairs. Bad Faults: Kinks in the tail, incorrect eye color or color of paw pads and nose leather. White lockets or buttons. Long coat or any coarseness of the coat. Coat color not chestnut to the roots.

Remarks: To want a Havana, whether of the British or American type, you must obviously like the chestnut color. Beyond this, the breed exhibits all of the features associated with the Siamese, these being a little less obvious in the Havana Brown of the USA. The short coat is easily managed — just a quick daily polishing to keep up the high gloss appearance. The breed does not enjoy undue popularity on either side of the Atlantic so is very much one for the specialist.

HIMALAYAN

The pointed Persian is one in which the bodily extremities are colored, while the body is a complementary diluted shade of the pointed color. The heavily pigmented areas are the mask, legs, feet and tail. There may be some darker shading on the body, but, if it is allowed, it must never be excessive. The pattern's origins were crosses between Persians and Siamese in order to establish pattern, followed by careful breeding so as to remove all trace of the Siamese type. The main colors are listed below. This cat is referred to as the Himalayan breed by some registries.

COLOURPOINT LONGHAIR

HISTORY: The Himalayan is a hybrid created by crossing the Siamese with the Persian. The ultimate result is a Persian with the colored points of a Siamese. The first attempts at producing this breed were made in Sweden and the USA during the 1920s. Efforts continued into the 1930s, but success was limited and seems to have died out. However, in 1947 the well-established Siamese breeder Brian Sterling-Webb happened to see a colorpointed longhaired cat which was the result of chance breeding. He decided to produce a similar cat but with longer hair. It took eight years of dedicated breeding before the GCCF in Great Britain recognized the new breed, which was called the Colourpoint Longhair. The name has been retained to this day in Great Britain and most other countries.

HIMALAYAN, "FLAME POINT"

HIMALAYAN, SEAL POINT
Male, Quadruple Champion

By 1950 a few breeders in the USA were again trying to produce the longhaired colorpoint. In Canada, English imports were shown during 1957, and by 1961 most American registries had recognized the breed, but under the name of Himalayan. In 1983 the CFA decided that the Himalayan should be regarded as a color variant of the Persian, which it thus became from 1984.

The breed is interesting because while Himalayan x Himalayan pairings are still popular, it is found that in order to maintain quality of type (conformation) there is a need to mate Himmies to good Persians. Such matings do not produce Himalayans at the first generation, because all of the kittens will be self colored black, blue or whatever (depending on the colors of the Himalayan and the Persian parents). However, all of the kittens will carry the recessive gene for Himalayan. When such a kitten is paired to a Himalayan, the theoretical results are 50% Himalayan and 50% self Persian, but carrying the Himalayan gene. The CFA, in its annual list of registrations, distinguishes between visual Himalayans and colorpoint carrier cats.

From the foregoing it will be appreciated that breeding quality Himalayans is not as easy as breeding in most other cats. Not only must quality be attained but, in achieving this, a number of non-Himalayan kittens will be produced. These will of course be Persians, but may not actually be true selfs because they may not be homozygous for their color. A sound basic understanding of color inheritance is thus definitely a useful, if not obligatory, attribute of the Himalayan breeder.

ALLOWABLE OUTCROSSES: Persian

HIMALAYAN, CREAM POINT
Female

HIMALAYAN, RED POINT
Female

RECOGNITION

All associations recognize the colorpoint long-hair, it being a case of the status they accord to it. This will be one of the following:

1. As the breed Himalayan. In this instance it will be seen in all of the colors accepted within the Persian breed as colorpoints.

2. As a color variety of the Persian. In this status the various colors are listed along with all other colors and patterns. Alternatively, it will be regarded as a color class (Himalayan) in its own right.

HIMALAYAN, SEAL POINT

HIMALAYAN, BLUE POINT
Female, Kitten

3. As the breed Colourpoint Longhair in the UK and many other countries. All of the available colors are then varieties of the Colourpoint Longhair breed.

DESCRIPTION

The Himalayan is judged according to the Persian standard to which you are referred in respect of bodily conformation.

Eyes: Deep vivid blue is preferred to lighter shades of blue.

Color: In order to be totally inclusive the following are those accepted by the GCCF (GB). Other associations may not accept all of these colors, but will no doubt do so in due course.

COLOR POINTS	BODY
Seal	Cream-white
Blue	Glacial white
Chocolate	Ivory-white
Red (Flame)	Apricot-white
Cream	Cream-white

HIMALAYAN, CREAM POINT
Male, Kitten

HIMALAYAN, BLUE POINT
Female, Champion

HIMALAYAN, SEAL LYNX POINT

Tortiepoints: The points are seal, blue, chocolate or lilac broken with shades of red or cream. Body color as in the solid colorpoints.

Tabbypoints: Clearly defined 'M' on the forehead. Spectacle markings around eyes, spotted whisker pads. Broken rings around front legs. Rear legs barred on front upper leg and thigh. Tail broken ringed. Inner ear fur and tufts a lighter shade. Paw pads and eye rims to tone with points.

Seal on pale brown agouti	*Cream-white*
Blue on light beige agouti	*Glacial white*
Chocolate on light bronze agouti	*Ivory white*
Lilac on pale beige agouti	*Magnolia-white*
Red on apricot agouti	*Apricot-white*
Cream on paler cream agouti	*Cream-white*

HIMALAYAN, RED POINT
Quadruple Grand Champion

Tortie Tabbypoints: Normal tabby pattern patched with red or cream. The extent of the tortie is not important as long as both elements (tortie and tabby) are clearly visible. There are four tortie tabbypoints: Seal, blue-cream, chocolate and lilac. The body color corresponds to that indicated for the tabbypoints. In the dilute colors, such as lilac and blue-cream, the tabby markings will be less evident than in the darker shades, such as seal or blue.

Bad Faults: White toes, any eye color other than blue, lack of contrast between colorpoints and body color, incorrect pigment color in pads, nose leather and eye rims.

HIMALAYAN, TORTIE POINT
Female

HIMALAYAN, BLUE POINT
Male

HIMALAYAN, BLUE POINT
Female

HIMALAYAN, BLUE POINT
Male, Champion

Remarks: Irrespective of whether it is a color variety of the Persian, or a breed in its own right, the Himalayan will always appeal to those who admire the Persian, but like the Siamese (or Himalayan) pattern. The breed is a large well muscled cat, but its dense and long coat will definitely need daily grooming, otherwise its gorgeous look will be replaced by a tangled mess! A challenging choice for the breeder/exhibitor, or simply a very impressive pet around the home.

HIMALAYAN, PERSIAN/TORTOISESHELL
HYBRID
Female, Kitten

HIMALAYAN, TORTIE POINT
Female

HIMALAYAN, SEAL POINT

JAPANESE BOBTAIL

HISTORY: The mutation that creates reduced tail length in this breed, while not common, is not unique. It appears from time to time in numerous countries. In this particular breed it is of Far Eastern origin, specifically, Japan. Credit for the breed's development and recognition goes to a Mrs. Freret, who imported a trio of Bobtails from Japan in 1968. The Bobtail gained full status with the CFA in 1976. The breed is often depicted with a welcoming raised paw, a good luck sign associated with these cats in Japan. The bobtail of this breed, unlike the stumpies produced by the British Manx cat, is not associated with any known abnormality. This is not always understood and may have influenced the fact that the breed has not enjoyed the popularity it really deserves. The tail is the result of a recessive mutation (compared to the dominant in the Manx). This means that both of a cat's genes are for the bobtail if this is exhibited, whereas in the Manx the double dominant is a lethal situation. If a Bobtail is mated to a normal- tailed cat, all of the kittens will be bobtail carriers, though having a normal-length tail themselves.

JAPANESE BOBTAIL, "MI-KE" (TRICOLOR)

JAPANESE BOBTAIL, BROWN MACKEREL
TABBY AND WHITE
Male

ALLOWABLE OUTCROSSES: None.

RECOGNITION: All American associations. Not recognized in the UK.

DESCRIPTION

Head: When viewed from the front the head forms a triangle. The cheekbones are set high and the muzzle is of moderate length, having a whisker break. The facial expression is soft and not at all Siamese.

Ears: Large, wide at their base, set far apart, but at right angles to the head rather than flaring outwards.

Eyes: Large, oval more than round in shape, they help give the breed its gorgeous facial expression. They should never bulge from the cheekbones or forehead. Their color should be appropriate to the coat color.

Body: Medium in size, long and lean. Never too cobby or overlong, the body is muscular without being rounded.

Legs & Feet: Long and slender, the hind legs are longer than those of the front. However, in normal stance the hind legs are bent such that the body stays in an almost horizontal position. The front legs are straight and in line with the shoulders. The paws are oval and neat.

Tail: This may vary from one individual to another but the following is an overall requirement. It is composed of one or more curves, bends or kinks. The furthest extension of the tail must be no more than three inches from the tail base. The direction of the tail in relation to

JAPANESE BOBTAIL, BLACK AND WHITE
Male, Champion

JAPANESE BOBTAIL, "MI-KE"
Female

the body is of no importance. The tail is well covered with fur and may appear as a pom-pom.

Coat: Described as medium in length, it is short by most people's understanding of coat lengths. Fine and silky in texture, there is a lack of a noticeable underfur, so the coat lays flat to the body. It is somewhat longer on the tail.

Color: Any color and pattern is permitted excepting, in some associations, the Siamese pattern or agouti ticked pattern as displayed by the Abyssinian breed. The most popular colors are the bicolors and tricolors. In Japan, the tricolors, known as Mi-Ke, are considered to be good luck charms. Preference is given to bold dramatic markings and rich, vivid colors.

Bad Faults: Short round head, cobbyness, tail bone absent or extending too far from body. Tail lacking fluffy appearance or pom-pom.

Delayed bobtail effect, which means a tail with close-lying hair preceding the pom-pom.

Remarks: The Japanese Bobtail is a truly delightful feline that combines a really cute appearance with an easy-to-manage coat. At first, the short tail may look unusual, but it is surprising how soon you come to find it very appealing.

"Mi-ke" (Tricolor) Japanese Bobtail. Photo by Isabelle Francais.

JAPANESE BOBTAIL, "MI-KE" (TRICOLOR)
Female Kitten

JAPANESE BOBTAIL, WHITE
Female, Kitten

Japanese Bobtail. Photo by Isabelle Francais.

KORAT

HISTORY: This breed is termed a natural breed of a province of Thailand. Although it is thought to have existed for a number of centuries, it did not reach the Western cat world until 1896, when the owner of a cat exhibited as a blue Siamese in London insisted it was not a Siamese but a true blue breed quite distinct from the Siamese. Nothing more appears on the breed until it was introduced to the USA in 1959. It gained recognition with most American registries in the period 1965-69 but had to wait until 1975 in Great Britain.

In its homeland, where it is called the Si-Sawat, it is regarded as a good luck cat. The Thai name means a mingled color of gray and light green.

ALLOWABLE OUTCROSSES: None.

RECOGNITION: All associations.

DESCRIPTION

Head: When viewed from the front the head is heart shaped, a characteristic feature of the breed. In profile there is a slight stop at the junction of the nose and forehead. The forehead is large and flat and there is plenty of breadth between the eyes. The muzzle is neither pointed nor square but is gently curved.

Ears: Set high on the head and with a taper to a nicely rounded tip. The hair on the inner ear is sparse.

Eyes: Large and luminous, they appear over-large in relation to the size of the face. Their color is luminous green but an amber cast is acceptable. In kittens the color is yellow to amber-green and does not fully develop until maturity.

Body: Semi-cobby, neither too compact nor especially svelte. When viewed from the front the chest is wide and the legs set well apart. The back exhibits a smooth curve.

Legs & Feet: Well proportioned and such that the overall length of the cat from nape of neck to base of tail is about the same as the height from the tail base to the floor. Paws oval and compact.

Tail: Medium in length and tapering to a rounded tip.

Coat: Short to medium in length, glossy and lying close to the body. When on the move, or bending forward, the fur of the spine tends to break.

Color: Any shade of blue, tipped with silver, the more tipping the better. There should be no

KORAT, BLUE
Female

shading or tabby markings. If the tipping is restricted to the head and legs, this is undesirable. The tipping is apparent throughout the cat's development and reaches its best once the cat is mature at about two years old. Paw pads and nose leather are dark blue ranging to lavender.

Bad Faults: Kink in tail, white buttons or locket, incorrect eye color in adult, and any color other than silver blue.

Remarks: If you like blue cats, then the Korat is certainly worth considering. It is not an especially popular breed—indeed, must be regarded as quite rare — but enjoys the support of a very dedicated group of breeders. While its numbers have declined over the years with the largest registry, they have increased in Great Britain, where the breed was 16th in the rankings in 1990.

KORAT, BLUE
Female

MAINE COON

HISTORY: There are numerous folk stories that tell of the origins of the Maine Coon. One is they are the result of crossings with raccoons (thus the Coon part of their name), while another is that they are hybrids of cats and bobcats. Of course, neither of these is true. Another, more plausible, story relates that they are the direct descendants of six cats shipped to the USA by Marie Antoinette shortly before she 'lost her head' during the French Revolution. Again, this adds spice to the tales that surround the breed, but should be taken as part of the folklore of the Maine Coon.

The reality is that the breed is almost certainly the result of natural hybridization between American shorthairs and any of the longhaired cats that were imported into the USA from Europe during the early years of the 18th century, possibly even some years prior to this. Such matings are unlikely to have been deliberate, but the result was that a quite distinctive type of cat emerged in the New England states. It possessed all of the qualities needed by a cat that had to endure harsh winters and a life often spent living off the land in and around farming communities.

If the American Shorthair is regarded as an English cat that settled to become an American, then the Maine Coon can claim to be the first, thus oldest, all-American breed. Once established, by the mid-1850s, it is quite possible that it received further infusions of longhaired genes from Turkish cats. The latter, along with Persians, were to become very fashionable by the turn of the 20th century. Indeed, so popular did the Persians become that the Maine Coon all but died out.

It is known that as early as the 1860s farmers exhibited their cats at local fairs, but of course these were very informal affairs — there were no cat clubs and organizing bodies at that time. When the first official American cat show took place in Madison Square Garden in 1895 it heralded a new era in cat ownership. In the same year a Maine Coon took top honors in a New York cat show. It was this breed that was

MAINE COON, SILVER MACKEREL TABBY
Male Grand Champion

MAINE COON, BLUE CLASSIC TABBY
Male

best cat in the Boston shows of 1897-99, but the decline then set in. With the desire to own Persians, Siamese, and other exotics, the public largely forgot the hardy all-American that had served farmers and townspeople for so many years. In barely a decade from 1895, the Maine Coon had virtually disappeared from the show scene.

In 1953 the Central Maine Coon Cat Club was formed by a number of dedicated breeders concerned to revive the country's oldest breed (and first show cat). They held their own shows and encouraged the breeding and improvement of the Maine Coon. It seems quite amazing that it was not until 1967 that this very old American breed would gain recognition by a number of cat associations in the USA. The CFA did not recognize the breed until 1976. The reason for this long delay in acceptance of the breed was due to the fact that breeders did not draw up an agreed standard until 1967. In 1968 the Maine Coon Breeders and Fanciers Association was formed to foster the interests of the breed and from that date the breed has steadily 'clawed' its way back into the hearts of Americans. Indeed, in the 1988 GCCF standard of the UK, the Maine Coon (along with the Exotic Shorthair) finally also gained preliminary recognition in Great Britain. This was a rare honor, for these were thus the first American breeds to gain such status.

ALLOWABLE OUTCROSSES: None.

RECOGNITION: All Associations.

DESCRIPTION

Head: Of rounded shape when viewed from the front, but not like that of the Persian. In profile the shade is wedged, but not excessively so. The muzzle is well developed and the nose should form a straight line with the chin, giving a square-like look. The cheek bones are set high and are well filled. The nose is straight, but with a slight concave at the nasal bridge. There is no definite stop, but a curve from nose to forehead.

Ears: Of generous size, wide at their base and tapering to a point. Set high on the head and well apart. They are well tufted with hair, which is a distinct feature of the breed.

Eyes: Large and rounded. Set at a very slight inclination towards the ears. Color may be green gold or copper, though white cats may be blue or odd-eyed (one blue one another color). There is no relationship between eye and coat colors.

Body: This is a medium to large sized cat which should display good muscle and width of chest. The body is basically a rectangle, neither overlong nor with any tendency to look square.

Legs & Feet: Of medium length and of substance that befits

MAINE COON, BROWN CLASSIC TABBY
Male

MAINE COON, BROWN CLASSIC TABBY
Male

a rugged breed. The paws are large, rounded and well tufted with hair. Five toes on front feet, four on rear — this being standard to any cat.

Tail: Long, thick at base and tapering to its extremity. The fur is very full, giving a plume-like appearance that is characteristic of the breed.

Coat: The Maine Coon is a breed that must be capable of surviving very bad weather — hot, cold or wet. To achieve this the coat must be heavy, silky and with a good underfur. The topcoat should lay flat to the body. The overall appearance is described as shaggy due to the differing hairlengths. There is a pronounced frontal ruff, or bib, and the breeches are well furred. The mask hair is short, but longer on the rear of the cheeks. The stomach and flanks sport long hair, but it should not be excessively so.

In warmer climates the breed will lose fur during the summer months, though the plume-like tail fur will remain. The coat should never appear dense and woolly as seen in Persians. This would greatly detract from the essence — and practicality — of this hardy breed.

MAINE COON, BROWN CLASSIC TORBIE
Female, Kitten

Color: The original color of the Maine Coon was tabby. Today the breed is seen in every possible color and pattern other than pointed and its related solid colors of chocolate and lilac. These will no doubt appear in due course. The present colors allowed are as follows. Not all of these colors are accepted, at this time, by any one association. Others are being added to the list each year.

MAINE COON, SILVER CLASSIC TABBY
Female, Kitten

MAINE COON, RED CLASSIC TABBY AND
WHITE
Male

SOLID COLORS

White: Pure glistening white. Paw pads and nose leather pink.

Black: Dense coal black from roots to tip. Ideally, the fur must be free of any tendency to have a smoke colored underfur, or any rusty brown look to the topcoat. This is extremely difficult to achieve, which is why dense black coats are both scarce and highly prized. Black is a 'color' that takes time to mature, so kittens may display a brass or rusty looking color which will darken with maturity. Paw pads and nose leather black or brown.

Blue: The color should be as even as possible. Paw pads and nose leather blue.

Red: Deep and rich. No shading or ticking. Paw pads and nose leather brick red.

Cream: Even shade of buff cream free of

markings or ticks. Paw pads and nose leather pink.

TABBY COLORS (MACKEREL OR CLASSIC)

Brown Tabby: Black markings on copper agouti ground. Paw pads and nose leather black or brown.

Blue Tabby: Blue markings on beige agouti ground. Paw pads and nose leather blue (GCCF), old rose (CFA).

Red Tabby: Rich red markings on apricot agouti ground. Paw pads and nose leather deep pink (GCCF) brick red (CFA).

Cream Tabby: Rich cream markings on cooler cream agouti ground. Paw pads and nose leather pink.

Tortie Tabby: Black markings on a warm copper agouti ground which is overlaid with shades of red. Paw pads and nose leather black and/or pink.

MAINE COON, BROWN CLASSIC TABBY
Male, Double Grand Champion

MAINE COON, SILVER MACKEREL TABBY
Male, Double Grand Champion

Blue Tortie Tabby: Blue markings on soft beige agouti ground which is overlaid with shades of cream. Paw pads and nose leather blue and/or pink.

Silver: Blue silver: Red silver: Cream silver:

Tortie silver & Blue tortie silver tabbies: As above but on a silver agouti ground. Paw pads and nose leather as appropriate to the color of the markings.

SHADED AND SMOKE COLORS

All solid and tortoiseshell colors are accepted. The underfur should be as white as possible, with the darker points being most clear on the back head and feet. In the shaded colors the appearance should produce a mantle over the back. In the smoke colors the white underfur is not apparent until the fur is parted or when the cat is in motion.

Black Smoke	Black Shaded
Blue Smoke	Blue Shaded
Red (Cameo) Smoke	Red (Cameo) Shaded
Cream Smoke	Cream Shaded
Tortie Smoke	Tortie Shaded
Blue-Cream Smoke	Blue-cream shaded

MAINE COON, BROWN CLASSIC TABBY
Kitten

Golden Smoke
Golden Chinchilla
Red Chinchilla
   (Shell Cameo)

Blue Tortie Shaded
Silver Chinchilla
Silver Shaded

of white is a matter of chance not within the control of the breeder.

Bad Faults: Cobby body shape (too square in appearance), blue or odd-eye color other than in whites, more than one third of the fur white in bi- or particolors (GCCF), an even coat length (one lacking in a ruff or good flank length), and fine boned.

BICOLOR AND PARTICOLOR

Any solid color, tortoiseshell, shaded or smoke color, and white. The base color should predominate, but it is preferred that there be some white on the mask, chest, stomach, legs and feet. However, any cat showing less than the preferred extent of white, but which is otherwise an excellent cat, should not be unduly discriminated against, because the extent

MAINE COON, BROWN MACKEREL TABBY
Male

Remarks: This is one of the truly gorgeous cat breeds. It is perhaps fitting that after being neglected for so long it now probably ranks fourth most popular show cat in the USA. Its fur is manageable, but really needs grooming every other day to keep it looking and feeling sleek. It is a very hardy breed well able to fend for itself — but it would obviously prefer to enjoy the creature comforts of its owner's home, which it usually gets.

MAINE COON, BROWN CLASSIC TABBY AND WHITE
Male, Double Grand Champion

MANX

HISTORY: The origins of the Manx, or tailless cat, as it has become known, have never been documented. Some say it is of Spanish origin and arrived on the British island by swimming ashore from one of the defeated Armada ships in 1588. Others say it developed from a British Shorthair mutation on the island itself, while others claim it came via trading ships from the Orient. The British Shorthair seems the most likely ancestor, given that the breed only came into prominence during the 19th century.

Although thought of as tailless, a number of examples do, in fact, have tails. The show specimen must be tail-free, displaying a slight indentation where the tail bone would normally be found. The gene that causes this condition in the breed is a dominant that is lethal in the homozygous (double) state and can cause various problems, even in the single state.

The Manx people are very proud of their tailless cats. The Manx is featured on their stamps, coins, and, of course, in gift stores. It has done much, along with the famed TT motorcycle races, to promote this little island just off the coast of England. The breed is not very popular in Britain, but since its arrival in the USA early in this century it has built up a steady following, and ranks in the top 15 or so most popular breeds with the CFA.

MANX, BROWN CLASSIC TABBY
Triple Grand Champion

MANX, BLACK AND WHITE BICOLOR
Male

ALLOWABLE OUTCROSSES: None.

RECOGNITION: All associations.

DESCRIPTION

Head: Large and almost round, with full cheeks. The nose is broad, straight, of medium length and without noticeable break as it curves into the forehead. The muzzle should display no indication of snipyness. The neck is short and powerful.

Ears: Tallish and set high on the head with a slight outward angle. Open at their base, they taper to a rounded tip.

Eyes: Large and round, they are slightly slanted towards the nose. The color should be appropriate to the coat color.

Body: Solid and compact. The chest is wide and the back relatively short and ending in a definite round rump. The rump should be higher than the shoulders. The flanks should display good depth. This is a well muscled cat that is quite heavy for its medium size.

Legs & Feet: The front legs are short and muscular, well set apart to allow for the ample chest. Those of the back are longer and with powerful thighs. The paws are round and neat.

Tail: Absolute taillessness is the desired state. There should be no bone or cartilage that would interfere with the roundness of the rump. Tails of various lengths can appear in litters and, depending on their size, are termed, riser, stubby, longy and normal — the tailless condition being known as rumpy. All Manx cats are obligate heterozygotes, meaning that they can only ever carry one gene for taillessness. A normal-tailed Manx cat produced in a litter, when mated to a Manx of similar genotype, cannot produce Manx cats, so the breeding of these felines is not without numerous problems: many offspring will be of no value whatsoever.

Coat: The coat is thick and resilient, having good undercoat over which is laid a sound topcoat of guard and awn hairs. The fur is glossy but hard rather than silky. The quality of the coat is of greater importance than its color or pattern, all other aspects of the cat being equal.

Color: In Great Britain all colors and patterns are accepted other than the pointed pattern (Siamese). In the USA chocolate, and lavender, as well as pointed pattern, are not permitted. Paw pads and nose leather colors are as for the coat color. The various colors are discussed under the Persian, American Shorthairs, and other breeds.

Bad Faults: A rise of bone or cartilage at the end of the spine. Lack of a double coat, weak chin, uneven bite and an abnormality of the spine, hind legs and toes.

Remarks: The Manx is a fascinating breed. However, would-be owners should discuss carefully the implications of the breed with their vet, especially if they intend to become breeders. This will save unnecessary heartache if kittens have to be destroyed because they are born with abnormalities associated with the tailless condition.

MANX, ODD-EYED WHITE
Female, Grand Champion

MANX, WHITE
Female, Kitten

MANX, BROWN CLASSIC TABBY
Male

MANX, BLACK AND WHITE
Male

NORWEGIAN FOREST

HISTORY: The origins of this very old natural breed are unknown. Some believe it is the result of crossings between British shorthairs and longhairs that were found throughout Europe from about the 16th century. It is said that British cats were taken by the Vikings to their Norwegian homelands. They became the local farm cats that would later mate with longhaired cats, also taken by the Vikings as they plundered the lands of Europe and the countries around the Mediterranean Sea. However, the breed could as easily have arrived in Norway via Russia, which has its own natural longhaired cats.

NORWEGIAN FOREST CAT, BROWN CLASSIC
TABBY AND WHITE
Male, Champion

Whatever the origins, the breed is certainly very old and its role was much the same over the centuries. It was a farm cat used to protect grain from the local rodent population. Its long shaggy coat provided excellent insulation against the rigors of the Scandinavian winters, which are colder than those found in New England, where its look-alike, the Maine Coon was developed. Maybe there is a connection between the breeds that is not generally appreciated.

The first exhibition in Norway that featured cats is thought to have taken place in 1933. It almost certainly featured examples of this breed — albeit in what would be termed foundation stock level. This means they were of a fixed type but had no pedigrees, so their ancestry could not be proven. The first Norwegian cat club was formed in 1938. The breed was among

NORWEGIAN FOREST CAT, BROWN CLASSIC TABBY
Female, Grand Champion

the first to gain official recognition. It was virtually unknown outside of Scandinavia until relatively recent years when it began to attract a small but dedicated band of followers. It is still a rare breed outside of its homeland because most Western countries have their own equivalent longhaired breed.

ALLOWABLE OUTCROSSES: None.

RECOGNITION: ACFA: TICA: CFF.

DESCRIPTION

The Norwegian Forest is very similar to the Maine Coon. As it is accepted in basically the same color range you are referred to that breed, which will provide a general guide to its looks. The available colors are not as extensive as in the Maine Coon at this time because the breed is nothing like as popular. These will appear as more breeders become captivated by the charm of this rugged cat.

NORWEGIAN FOREST CAT, BROWN
MACKEREL TABBY AND WHITE
Female

NORWEGIAN FOREST CAT, BROWN
MACKEREL TABBY AND WHITE
Male Champion.

NORWEGIAN FOREST CAT, RED MACKEREL
TABBY
Male

Bad Faults: See Maine Coon, as the breeds are essentially similar in the features that are considered undesirable.

Remarks: If you like a hardy, longhaired, unfashioned by humans, sort of cat then the Forest is certainly one of the obvious candidates. Its popularity in the USA and Great Britain will only be held in check because of the greater availability of the Maine Coon breed. Choose either because they are both super breeds.

NORWEGIAN FOREST CAT, BLUE MACKEREL
TABBY
Male

NORWEGIAN FOREST CAT, BROWN
MACKEREL TABBY AND WHITE
Female, Champion

NORWEGIAN FOREST CAT, SILVER
MACKEREL TABBY AND WHITE
Male, Kitten

NORWEGIAN FOREST CAT, BROWN
MACKEREL TABBY
Male

NORWEGIAN FOREST CAT, BROWN
MACKEREL TABBY AND WHITE
Male

NORWEGIAN FOREST CAT, BLUE MACKEREL
TABBY
Male

A gorgeous blue mackerel tabby with white strikes an attractive pose. Photo by Isabelle Francais.

NORWEGIAN FOREST CAT, BLACK
Female

NORWEGIAN FOREST CAT, BLUE TORBIE
AND WHITE
Female

Norwegian Forest Cat. Photo by Isabelle Francais.

OCICAT

HISTORY: One of the growing number of spotted domestic cats, the Ocicat was one of those chance happenings we all dream of. The original breeder, Virginia Daly, was trying to obtain Siamese with Abyssinian ticking on the points. The initial pairing resulted in all Abyssinian-marked kittens. However, when one of these was mated to a chocolate Siamese, among the desired litter was one gorgeously spotted kitten. A repeat mating produced the founding cats of the new breed.

Initially, outcrossings other than with Abyssinians and Siamese occurred. The American Shorthair was utilized to increase size and introduce extra colors, especially silver. The result of these pairings has been the development of a most beautiful breed, which gained recognition in 1987. It is not as yet accepted by all associations, the most notable absentee being the GCCF, but they will surely recognize the breed in due course.

ALLOWABLE OUTCROSSES: Abyssinian until 1995 (CFA).

OCICAT, SILVER SPOTTED TABBY
Male, Kitten

RECOGNITION: CFA; ACA: TICA.

DESCRIPTION

Head: A modified wedge showing a slight curve from muzzle to cheeks. There is no nose break, but a gentle rise from the nose to the forehead. The muzzle is broad and the whisker break is only moderate. In profile the head is of moderate length and is carried on an arched neck.

Ears: Medium in size and tapering to a rounded tip. They are set at approximately 45° to an imaginary line drawn across the brow. Ear tufts are a bonus if present.

Eyes: Large and almond shaped, they are set at a very slight angle towards the ears. There should be somewhat more than the length of an eye between the eyes. The eye color may be any color other than blue — though blue-eyed pets are very popular.

Body: Rather long bodied, but solid and of athletic appearance. Chest of moderate depth. The back level rises slightly from the shoulder to the rump. The torso should never look coarse and bulky.

Legs & Feet: Medium in length and well muscled, yet elegant. The paws are oval and compact.

Tail: Fairly long and medium to slim. There is a slight taper to the tip.

Coat: Short, fine in texture and with a lustrous sheen. Any suggestion of woolliness is a decided fault. The hair lies close to the body. It should be just long enough to accommodate the required amount of color banding. Color: The overall pattern of spots seen in the Ocicat is similar to that described for the Egyptian Mau. However, the range of colors accepted is much more extensive.

Spots & Markings	Ground Color (Agouti)	Paw Pads	Nose Leather
Tawny	Ruddy or Bronze	Black or Seal	Brick Red
Chocolate	Warm Ivory	Chocolate Pink	Pink
Cinnamon	Warm Ivory	Pink or Rose	Pink
Blue	Pale Blue or Buff	Blue	Blue
Lavender	Pale Buff or Ivory	Lavender-Pink	Pink
Fawn	Pale Ivory	Lavender-Pink	Pink
Black	Silver White	Black	Brick Red (Called Silver)

To each of the above colors there is silver shade, thus a chocolate silver, which is chocolate on a white agouti ground, cinnamon on white, blue, lavender, and a fawn — each on a white ground. Paw pads and nose leather colors are as in the appropriate color.

Bad Faults: Kinked tail, blue eyes, white lockets, coarseness of body.

Remarks: The Ocicat is a most impressive feline that is of good size. Named for the Ocelot, a small South American wild feline, the Ocicat is building up its numbers each year as it wins over more admirers, both for its looks and its reputed intelligence.

Oriental Longhair

HISTORY: the Oriental Longhair is one of the newer cat breeds. It is in all respects a longhaired version of the Oriental Shorthair. As with many other breeds that are duplicates of a breed seen in a shorthaired form, the source of the longhaired gene is rarely known for certain. In this instance, it may have been a natural mutation with the oriental breed, or may have been introduced from a breed such as the Balinese, and then the colorpoint pattern bred out to produce an attractive cat of Oriental conformation, but with a medium-long coat. The breed has only limited recognition at this time, but this situation will change with the passage of time.

ALLOWABLE OUTCROSSES: Oriental Shorthair.

RECOGNITION: TICA.

DESCRIPTION:

Head: Wedge shaped whether viewed from the front or in profile. The nose is straight with no break where it joins the forehead.

A pair of lovely Oriental Longhairs. Left: fawn mackerel tabby. Right: shaded chestnut spotted tabby. Photo by Isabelle Francais.

Ears: Large, their outer edges form part of the straight lines that create the triangular shape of the frontal view of the face. They are set wide apart and are open at their bases.

Eyes: Almond (Oriental) in shape, they exhibit a slant towards the nose.

Body: Long and svelte, the impression is of a very slim cat that should never appear coarse or stocky.

Legs & Feet: Slim in bone and of good length. The hind legs are longer that the front. The paws are small and oval.

Tail: Long and slim, the tail tapers to a rounded, not blunt, tip.

Coat: Although classed as a longhaired breed, the fur is very manageable, being of only medium length on the body, but long and plume-like on the tail. It is sufficiently long on the face to soften the expression when compared with the Oriental Shorthair. The texture is fine and silky, the coat lying close to the body and exhibiting minimal underfur.

Color: All colors are permitted other than the pointed pattern. At this time, all of the colors and patterns seen in the Oriental Shorthair may not be readily available in this breed but will be seen in due course. The eye color is a vivid green, other than in the white—in which case it will be blue, though green-eyed whites are permitted in the USA. Odd-eyed whites are not accepted.

Bad Faults: Kink in the tail, incorrect eye color, white buttons or lockets, and any movement away from the Oriental type.

Remarks: The Oriental Longhair is the obvious choice for those liking the Siamese personality but who prefer a non-pointed pattern and a cat that has sufficient fur to soften the extreme type characteristic of the Siamese. The breed is to the Oriental Shorthair what the Balinese is to the Siamese.

ORIENTAL LONGHAIR, CHOCOLATE
SPOTTED TABBY
Male, Kitten

ORIENTAL SHORTHAIR

HISTORY: The origins of the Oriental Shorthairs go back to the 1950s when English breeders were trying to produce the Havana, or chestnut-colored 'Siamese.' Once this was achieved other colors, commencing with the lilac, quickly followed. These self- colored cats were called Foreigns, thus Foreign black, Foreign blue and so on. As the years passed, other color patterns were added, such as the tabbies, the smokes, and the tortoiseshell. These were called Orientals. By the late 1970s and early 1980s, most associations had given full status to this new breed.

The Oriental Shorthair is thus a Siamese in non-pointed colors and patterns. The selfs, or single colors, are called Foreigns in England (but not in the USA), while all other patterned colors are called Oriental Shorthair (including the selfs in the USA). The Oriental is thus a hybrid breed in which the other shorthair breeds used to introduce color have been bred out in favor of the Siamese type.

ALLOWABLE OUTCROSSES: Siamese and Colorpoint Shorthair (CFA).

RECOGNITION: All associations.

DESCRIPTION

Head: When viewed from the front the head is a triangular shape. There is no whisker pinch, the line between nose and ears being   as

ORIENTAL SHORTHAIR, EBONY BLACK
Male, Kitten

ORIENTAL SHORTHAIR, CHESTNUT
Female

ORIENTAL SHORTHAIR, FROST
Female

straight as possible. In profile, the head is a wedge and of good length. The nose should be straight, with no break as it joins the forehead. The neck is long and slender.

Ears: Large, set well apart and open at their base. They are so positioned that they continue the line of the triangle when viewed from the front.

Eyes: Oriental (almond) in shape, they slant towards the nose. They should display no squint (cross-eyed).

Body: Long and svelte, medium in size and with a tight abdomen. This is a slim breed. The hips should never be wider than the shoulders. The body should have firm muscle without being bulky.

Legs & Feet: Long and slim, with the hind legs being longer than the front. Paws are small and oval.

Tail: Long, thin and tapering from base to tip, which should not be blunt.

Coat: Very short, fine in texture and glossy. With minimal under-fur, the coat lies very close to the body.

Color: The range of colors and patterns in this breed is very extensive, especially in Great Britain. The selfs include white, black, blue, lilac, havana (chestnut in the USA), cinnamon, red, cream, caramel and fawn. Each of the tabby patterns of spotted, classic, mackerel and ticked (Abyssinian) can be had in any of numerous colors. The torties are available in black, blue, chocolate, lilac and other color shades. The eye color is a vivid green, except in the white, which should have blue eyes in the UK, but may alternatively have green eyes in the USA. Odd-eyed whites are not permitted.

Bad Faults: Incorrect eye color, kinks in the tail, white markings other than any stated in a color standard, long or coarse coat.

Remarks: The Oriental Shorthair offers all of the characteristics associated with the Siamese, but in a whole range of non-pointed colors and patterns. The breed is said to be a little less vocal than its close cousin.

ORIENTAL SHORTHAIR, FAWN SPOTTED TABBY
Male, Grand Champion

ORIENTAL SHORTHAIR, BROWN
TABBY
Female, Kitten

ORIENTAL SHORTHAIR, RED AGOUTI TABBY
Male, Quadruple Grand Champion

ORIENTAL SHORTHAIR, WHITE
Male, Triple Grand Champion

ORIENTAL SHORTHAIR, TORTOISESHELL
Female, Grand Champion

ORIENTAL SHORTHAIR, SILVER MACKEREL
TABBY
Female, Kitten

ORIENTAL SHORTHAIR, CREAM SPOTTED
TABBY
Female

PERSIAN

HISTORY: As with all breed types that are known to have existed for a number of centuries, the origins of the Persian are undocumented. The generally held view is that the breed is the result of selective breeding from cats taken to Great Britain by returning soldiers and travelers to the Middle East. It is known that longhaired cats had existed in England and mainland Europe from at least the 16th century. Where the longhaired gene came from (geographically) is not known, nor, indeed, if all longhairs have a common lineage, or whether they are the result of two or more independent mutations for such hair at the same locus.

Whatever the case may be, the longhaired cats from the areas of Turkey and Persia were considered impressive enough to be taken back to France and England. When the first cat show was held in London in 1871 it featured Persians as well as a French African cat that was clearly also of Persian type. While the show stoppers were white Persians, another Persian that impressed was black, gray and white. In the early years of the breed it was not generally recognized that the cats labeled as Persians were actually two quite separate breeds. There were the Turkish cats that looked much as they do to this day, and there were the Persians with their more dense and woolly coats, rounder faces and generally somewhat more stocky conformation.

However, while today you would never mistake a Persian for a Turkish Angora or Van, things were not as simple during the 19th century. The Persian had not been fashioned to the present level, nor was its coat as profuse. Differences were thus not as easily seen between the two types, which were thus interbred. The fashion became (and remains) to produce

PERSIAN, BLACK AND WHITE
Female, Kitten

PERSIAN, BLACK AND WHITE BICOLOR
Male, Champion

cats with as much hair as possible. The result was that the Turkish (Angora) type lost favor, and the name Angora was dropped.

By the last decade of the 19th century, Americans became very interested in the Persian breed, so many cats were exported from England to form the foundation stock on which Americans were to successfully build. While in the USA the breed retained its Persian name, this was dropped in the UK. Each color variety was given breed status under the tag of Longhaired. A black Persian thus became the Longhaired black breed, the white became the Long-

haired white and so on. More recently (1988), the British reinstated the Persian name, but the standard of points within the color and pattern groups differs, though still adding up to 100 points. There is a general standard and then certain colors or patterns have a modified version of this, thus all varieties still retain breed status.

Over the years, the Persian has changed dramatically from its early type. This is certainly true in respect of its facial structure, coat quality, and fur density. You will see more variation in these than in any other breed.

Whether or not you find the extremes seen in the Persian attractive, the fact is the breed is the most popular show cat in the world. It has also influenced the production of other breeds, such as the Exotic Shorthair, and the Himalayan (if this is regarded as a separate breed). Whether or not it has be used in other breeds, either to introduce longhair, or certain colors, remains a bone of contention within some breeds.

ALLOWABLE OUTCROSSES: None.

RECOGNITION: All associations.

DESCRIPTION

Head: Large, round, and with great breadth of skull. The cheeks are round and full. The forehead, seen in profile, is also rounded. The jaws should be broad, powerful and reflecting a proper bite. Although the jaws should be level, it is a fact that in many examples the bite is undershot and the dental work incomplete. This is a direct result of the standard's requirement for a foreshortened nose, which is taken to extremes in some instances. The nose should be short, wide and with a definite stop (break). It is described as snub. The Peke-faced Persian, with a button nose, enjoys some popularity in the USA, but is not allowed in Great Britain because

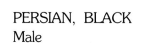

PERSIAN, BLACK
Male

of its obvious deleterious effect on the breathing and general well being of the cat. The neck is short and thick.

Ears: Small and round tipped, and set wide apart and low onto the head. The long fur of the head makes the ears appear smaller than they actually are. They should be well tufted.

Eyes: Large and round, they should neither bulge nor be sunken. Set far apart, their color will reflect the coat color. Most breeds feature copper colors, but the pointed breeds will be blue. Eye color is stated within the color descriptions.

Body: Medium or large in size, the general appearance is one of a cobby type cat set low on the leg. The chest is broad and deep, the shoulders and rump wide and well muscled. Although the various standards use the terms massive, great, and well muscled, in the breed description, the Persian is not an unduly heavy cat, nor as large as its appearance might suggest. Much of its bulk is made up of its generous coat.

Legs & Feet: Relatively short in relation to overall body size. Thick and strong. The paws are large, round, and well tufted with hair. The

PERSIAN, BLACK
Female

PERSIAN, BLACK
Female, Grand Champion

PERSIAN, BLACK
Male, Triple Grand Champion

forelegs should ideally be straight, not bowed.

Tail: Short and straight, but in a pleasing proportion to the body length. It should be carried at an angle lower than the back. Very well furred, thus bushy.

Coat: This, of course, is a feature of the breed. It should be long and dense. Its texture is fine but should not be unduly woolly. Some examples have a more silky texture than others, reflecting the origins of the breed and its association with the much more silky fur of the Turkish breeds. The neck ruff should be very generous and extend into the chest, between the front legs. All three hairs types should be present.

Color: Depending on the association you choose to join, the Persian is accepted in very many colors ranging from about 51-87. This compares to only about 15 at the turn of the century. It illustrates the tremendous interest in color breeding evident in the cat fancy. The color of a Persian will often totally change its facial expression.

Compare the almost angelic look of a white Persian with that of a tortoiseshell, which often has a quite fierce look to it. This reflects not only the actual colors, but the effect the pursuance of these has had on conformation, an aspect not always fully appreciated.

In this section not every color is described,

PERSIAN, BLACK SMOKE
Male, Triple Grand Champion

PERSIAN, BLACK SMOKE
Female

because many are actually very similar. The main colors and patterns are included so you have a broad guide to availability. The full list accepted by your chosen registration body will be supplied to you if you request this from them. In some instances the color and pattern may correspond to one given another name by differing societies. It is not possible to compare all of these. They represent an area of the cat fancy that creates considerable difficulties for even the experienced cat fancier, let alone the novice. Here, I have used the CFA and the GCCF as my basic source of reference on all matters.

SOLID (SELF) COLORS

Black: One of the original Persian colors, this should be as dense as coal. The hairs should be black from root to tip. Kittens may have the odd white ticked hairs, but these should disappear as the cat matures. A rusty look to the color is undesirable but again may be seen in kittens. Once adult, sun will bleach the color. Dampness will cause it to lose density. For these reasons all longhaired black cats are difficult to maintain to a high standard. Do not use talcum powder when grooming, as this will give the coat a scurfy look to it. Blacks are more popular in

PERSIAN, BLACK
Male, Kitten

PERSIAN, BLUE SMOKE
Male, Grand Champion

the USA than in Great Britain. Some have taken the highest awards in the show ring. Eye color is brilliant copper or deep orange. Paw pads and nose leather black or brown.

White: This should be glistening white, free from any marks or shading, though kittens may exhibit some darker shading that should disappear as it matures. White Persians may exhibit one of three eye colors: Blue, orange, and odd eyed. Odd eyes are one blue eye and one orange. Blue-eyed whites are associated with deafness.

In one study, the number of deaf cats (37%) was slightly greater than the number of white cats with normal hearing (31%). In the same study, 7% of the cats that were deaf were orange-eyed whites. The condition may be unilateral or bilateral, the latter usually seen in odd-eyed cats on the same side as the blue eye.

Whites have been bred to an extremely high standard in the USA, where they are very popular. They tend to be more typey, with more depressed noses, than their British counterparts.

Blue: In the UK the color may range from pale to medium, both being treated equally. In the USA the lighter shades are preferred. The color must be even from root to tip. The blue color is created by the dilution gene being present in

PERSIAN, BLUE

PERSIAN, BLACK SMOKE
Male

PERSIAN, BLUE
Male, Kitten

double dose, so blue is a dilute black. British blues are extremely high quality, having had their own specialty club since 1901, making it the oldest longhaired cat club in the world. Many of Britain's top blues were exported to the USA during the first two decades of this century, so America also has many super blues that have been developed from the original stocks. Kittens are born with faint tabby markings which disappear over the first few months.

Red: A deep, rich red is preferred. As with all self colors it should be free of ticks or shadings.

The color was originally called orange when it was seen at the first cat shows of the 19th century. This was of a lighter shade than has been produced over the years by selective color breeding. The red as seen in Persians is a sex-linked color, which means that the sex of the cat needs to be considered when calculating theoretical   expectations   from   matings   involving

PERSIAN, TORTIE SMOKE
Female, Kitten

red. Most reds will have, to a greater or lesser degree, tabby markings on their head and legs. The amount of markings will be determined by the type of tabby that is being 'masked,' Abyssinian being the faintest. Eye color is a brilliant copper or deep orange. Paw pads and nose leather are brick red (USA) or deep pink (UK).

Cream: An even shade of buff cream (CFA), or pale to medium cream (GCCF). The original creams stemmed from reds that carried the genes for dilution, but this fact was not under-

PERSIAN, BLUE AND WHITE BICOLOR
Male

PERSIAN, BLUE TORTIE SMOKE
Female

PERSIAN, BLUE

stood. British breeders regarded such examples as 'sports' or freak oranges, and sold them cheaply as pets. Many were sent to the USA where the color was well liked. By the 1920s it was appreciated that the quality of the cream could be improved greatly by selective breeding, a fact that the Americans quickly grasped and worked on. Ghost tabby markings may be seen on the head and legs of dark creams, thus a pale to medium shade is preferred. Quality creams are very impressive and when mated to blues will produce the blue-cream (a female-only color) that is in fact a

PERSIAN, CREAM AND WHITE BICOLOR
Female

PERSIAN, CAMEO TABBY

dilute tortoiseshell. Eye color is brilliant copper or deep orange.Paw pads and nose leather are pink.

Chocolate: This is a medium to dark chocolate color that was a byproduct of producing the pointed Persian (Himalayan or Colourpoint Longhair). The color was thus introduced from the Siamese and is therefore one of the newer colors. It has been greatly improved over the years. Though the standard calls for no shading, this will invariably be seen to some degree on the back, legs, and the mask. The chocolate Persian is known as the Kashmir in a couple of the American registries and as a self Himalayan by those who recognize the Kashmir as a separate breed. Its genetic base is that of a mutation which reduces the strength of the black melanin to brown — as compared to the blue in

PERSIAN, BLUE CREAM

PERSIAN, CREAM
Male

PERSIAN, CREAM

which the arrangement of the cells are such as to create the illusion of blue. Eye color brilliant copper or deep orange. Paw pads and nose leather are chocolate.

Lilac: This is described as warm in tone by the GCCF, and as a rich, warm lavender with a pinkish tone by the CFA. The color, genetically, is a dilute chocolate. The dilution genes were probably introduced from blue Persians. Like the chocolate, the

lilac Persian is sometimes referred to as a Kashmir or a self Himalayan. Eye color is brilliant copper or deep orange. Paw pads and nose leather are pink.

Smoke Colors

The smoke color pattern is created by the fur having a white base and the rest of the hair containing pigment. The white is seen only when the cat is moving. The coat does vary in the

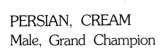

PERSIAN, CREAM
Male, Grand Champion

amount of dark pigment it contains and is darkest on the mask, back and feet. This accounts for the phrase 'a cat of contrasts' used in the standard of the GCCF. The color's genetic base is that inhibitor genes suppress the amount of pigment in the hair shaft, but not in a uniform manner. Smoke is a very old color pattern that had its own color class in the UK as long ago as 1893. The smokes in the red series (thus creams, torties and tabbies) are often referred to as being cameos.

Black Smoke: Body black shading to silver on sides and flanks.

PERSIAN, SHADED GOLDEN

PERSIAN, RED
Male

Blue Smoke: Body blue shading to silver on side and flanks.

Red (Cameo) Smoke: Body red shading to white on sides and flanks.

Tortie (Cameo) Smoke: Tipping to be of red, black or cream, well broken into patches.

Cream (Cameo) Smoke: Body cream shading to white on sides and flanks.

Blue-Cream (Cameo) Smoke: In the UK the tipping of blue and cream should be softly intermingled. In the USA the colors should form quite distinct patches. Blue-creams are always females.

Chocolate Smoke: Body chocolate shading to silver on the sides and flanks.

PERSIAN, RED
Male, Triple Grand Champion

PERSIAN, RED
Female

PERSIAN, RED CLASSIC TABBY
Female

Lilac Smoke: Body lilac shading to silver on the sides and flanks.

Chocolate Tortie Smoke: Body chocolate and shades of red broken into patches, shading to silver on the sides and flanks. Face and feet to show patches of chocolate and red. This color is always a female.

Lilac Tortie Smoke: Lilac and cream intermingled, shading to silver on the sides and flank. Face lilac and cream intermingled. This color is always a female.

The eye color in all smoke colors is a brilliant copper or deep orange. Paw pads and nose leather color should complement the basic color.

SHADED COLORS
The shaded color pattern is created in the

PERSIAN, CHINCHILLA SILVER

PERSIAN, CHINCHILLA SILVER
Female

same way as the smoke, but the tipping to the hairs is less extensive. The effect is that the shaded pattern results in a lighter color, the two colors being visible and producing a very attractive feline.

Red (Cameo) Shaded: White with red shading. Red most distinct on the mask, back, tail, legs and feet.

Tortie (Cameo) Shaded: Black, red and cream broken into patches over a white hair base. The face to carry the colors in a distinctive manner.

Golden Shaded: The hair base color is a rich warm cream, while the tipping is black. Eye color blue or blue-green. Paw pads black. Nose leather deep rose.

Silver Shaded: The hair base is white, while the tipping is black to create a dark silver effect. Eye color is green or blue-green. Paw pads black. Nose leather red. The eye color of the shaded silver is the clearest distinguishing feature between this color and the very similar pewter, whose eyes are copper or orange.

Pewter: The base hair color is white. This is evenly shaded with black to create the pewter appearance. Paw pads black or brown. Nose leather brick red outlined with black. Easily confused with the shaded silver, but distinguished from it by its orange or copper colored eyes.

SHELL COLORS

The shell color pattern is the lightest of the trio of color-tipped hair types. Only the very tips of the hair shafts carry darker pigment and the results are often exquisite. The shell pattern is also known as Chinchilla in certain colors.

Shell Cameo (Red Chinchilla): The hair base color is white, while the tips of the hair on the face, back, tail and flanks are red.

Chinchilla: The hair base color is pure white with just the tips being black on the face, back, tail and flanks. This color is also known as the silver Persian.

Chinchilla Golden: Base hair color rich warm cream (CFA) or apricot (GCCF) shaded with seal brown or black tipping. The effect of the tipping is to produce a darker color than the equivalent silver Chinchilla. Eye color green or blue-green. Paw pads brown or black, nose leather brick red.

Shell Tortoiseshell: The hair base color is white and the tipping is black with well defined patches of red and cream.

PERSIAN, SHADED SILVER

PERSIAN, SHADED SILVER
Male, Champion

It is highly probable that other chinchilla colors, such as blue, chocolate, and lilac, will make their appearance in due course, the blue already having been occasionally produced. All of the shaded colors will appear darker as kittens because the first part of the hair shaft to emerge will of course be the pigmented part. This will often show a tabby pattern that will be lost as the hairs gain length. The pattern becomes so distorted as not to be evident at all.

lated in any precise manner. There is thus an element of luck in producing show standard examples.

The original hope was that a cat with markings similar to those seen in the Dutch breed of rabbit could be achieved. The rabbit breeders attained this goal, though much of their stock will be mismarked, but it proved too much for cat breeders.

As the standards of the USA and Great Britain

PERSIAN, CALICO
Female, Kitten

BICOLORS

Although bicolored longhaired cats have been around for very many years, it has only been since the 1960s that they have been recognized as a variety of the Persian. Initially, the standards were far to difficult for breeders to reach in relation to the placement of the white, so they were rewritten to allow greater flexibility. Even so, many bicolors that are bred will fall short of the requirements and be of little exhibition value, though still be useful for breeding. This is because the genes controlling the amount and distribution of white cannot be manipu-

differ somewhat in defining the requirements of the bi- or two-colored cat, those of the CFA and GCCF are quoted exactly. The CFA states 'As a preferred minimum, the cats should have white feet, undersides, chest and muzzle. Less than this minimum should be penalized proportionately. Inverted 'V' on face desirable.' The GCCF states 'Any solid color and white, the patches of color to be clear, even and well distributed. Not more than two-thirds of the cat's coat to be coloured and not more than one-half to be white. Face to be patched with colour and white.'

The eye color should be brilliant copper or deep orange. The available colors are: black and white, blue and white, chocolate and white, lilac and white, red and white, cream and white.

In the USA the Persian Van bicolor is seen. This is a white cat which has the color confined to the head, tail and legs as seen in the Turkish Van breed. The present colors are red, blue, or cream — each with white. One or two small colored patches on the body are allowed.

TORTOISESHELL COLOR

This color has been seen since the latter 19th century and was probably derived from crosses between self Persians and tortie British shorthairs. It is, for all

PERSIAN, TORTOISESHELL
Female, Grand Champion

practical purposes, a female-only variety, any males produced being genetic abnormals, as they are in all the sex-linked red colors. Invariably they are sterile. Torties in any of the pet animals (rabbits, guinea pigs, hamsters) never enjoy tremendous popularity because they are difficult to produce and have been overshadowed by the more appealing tortie and whites, as well as the plethora of other colors produced over the years.

CALICO (TORTOISESHELL AND WHITE)

This color was originally called Chintz in Britain and, although it is an old variety, it had to wait a long time for official recognition. The term calico is used quite a lot in the USA for any tortoiseshell and white animal, such as goldfish, hamsters, rabbits and so on. It is derived from the printed cotton of a similar color that has been produced in India and other Asiatic countries for many centuries.

PERSIAN, COPPER-EYED WHITE

In the USA the colors are black with clearly defined patches of red and cream. A blaze of red and cream on the face is preferred. In Britain the three colors should be well broken into patches, this also applying to the facial hairs. Other than the shaded and blue-cream torties already discussed, there is also a chocolate tortie in which this color replaces the black. Eye color in the torties is brilliant copper or deep orange.

The pattern is tortoiseshell with white being interdispersed over the body in a well distributed manner. The standard of the CFA calls for a preferred minimum of white, which is as given for the bicolors. Calicos are always gorgeous-looking animals, it being a case that some are prettier than others. It is a female-only variety. Producing well-marked individuals is never easy. Nor can they be anticipated due to the random nature of the genes for white spotting (which is what white areas on cats are called). There are two other calico colors now accepted in Britain. They are the chocolate tortie and white, and the lilac tortie and cream. In each case the color named replaces the black in the coat. The lilac is of course a dilution of the chocolate, and the cream is the red diluted. The eye color is deep orange or brilliant copper.

PERSIAN, TORTOISESHELL
Female, Kitten

PERSIAN, BLUE-EYED WHITE
Female

RAGDOLL

HISTORY: The Ragdoll was developed in California during the 1960s. It is one of the few cat breeds that were ever trademarked. There are those that can be registered with the International Ragdoll Cat Association, which is a trademark, and those that can be registered with other cat registries and which can compete in major cat shows. The breed was developed from crosses involving a blue-eyed white female and, one would assume from their appearance, Birmans, Himalayans, bicolors, and similar cats that could introduce the desired color genes exhibited by the breed in its three varieties.

It is said that the Ragdoll is so named because of its ability to go floppy when handled. It is also credited with attributes that are extremely doubtful and potentially harmful to its welfare. For example, it is said to have a very high tolerance to pain and enjoys being mauled. No cat enjoys pain. Tolerance to pain is an individual matter in cats and certainly not breed-related as it is in certain bull breeds of dog. These dogs have been selectively bred over the centuries by placing them in high pain situations — such as dog fighting. You do not acquire high pain thresholds in a few decades of breeding household pet cats! This aspect of the breed should be taken as nonsense, because it could lead to some owners actually causing their pets unnecessary suffering in the mistaken belief that their cat is in some way impervious to pain. Tall stories apart, the Ragdoll is a most attractive breed. It will certainly have appeal to many would-be catowners.

ALLOWABLE OUTCROSSES: None.

RECOGNITION: ACA, ACFA, TICA, CFF:,GCCF.

DESCRIPTION

Head: Medium to large, it is flat between the ears. Cheeks well developed, as is the rounded muzzle. The nose is of medium length and has

RAGDOLL, SEAL POINT
Male, Grand Champion

RAGDOLL, SEAL MITTED POINT
Male

a very gentle break at the forehead.

Ears: Set wide on the head, the ears are broad at the base and taper to a rounded tip. There are moderate furnishings in the ear.

Eyes: Large and oval, with a slant towards the ears. The color is blue — the deeper the better.

Body: Long and muscular. The chest is broad. The breed is slow to mature, taking up to three or maybe more years to fully develop.

Legs & Feet: Of medium bone and length, well muscled and looking very solid. The paws are large, rounded and tufted.

Tail: Long and with a slight taper towards the tip.

Coat: Of medium length, the coat is dense, and silky in texture. The fur is long on the neck, creating a frame for the face. Relatively shorter on the shoulders and longer on the back, sides, flanks and underparts. The tail is bushy. The coat length is seasonal so will be shorter in the warmer months.

Color: Four colors are recognized: seal, chocolate, blue, and lilac (frost in USA). Each of the colors is seen in the following three coat patterns:

Colorpoint: The color of the points (mask, ears, feet and tail) to be well defined. The mask covers the cheeks, whisker pads, nose, eyes and chin. Paw pads and nose leather to be the same color as the points. White anywhere is a fault. The body color will be a lighter shade of the points color and will be paler on the chest and underparts.

Mitted: This is the same as the colorpoint, but there is white on the chin, bib, chest and underbody. A narrow blaze of white on the nose is permitted. The two front feet are white, this

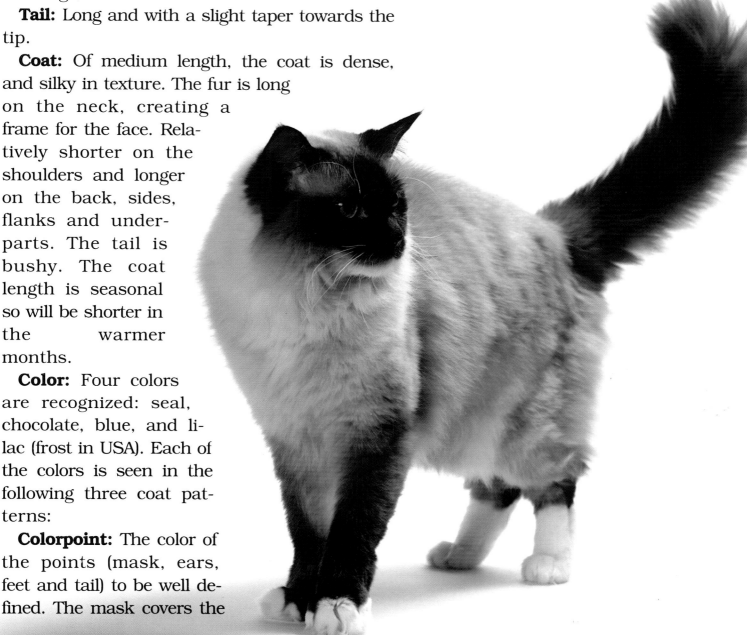

RAGDOLL, SEAL MITTED POINT
Male, Quadruple Grand Champion

not extending higher than the ankle. The rear feet are white, this extending no higher than the hock. Nose leather same color as points, paw pads pink.

Bicolor: Same as mitted but the face should have an area of white in the form of an inverted 'V.' This should commence on the forehead and pass over the nose and whisker pads to the chin. The front legs are all white. A limited amount of white may appear on the body but not on the points, other than where already

stated. Nose leather and paw pads will be pink.

Bad Faults: Kink in tail, leg bones too fine, round or too oriental-shaped eyes, narrow head, pale eye color, pronounced nose break.

Remarks: The Ragdoll makes an interesting addition to the longhaired breeds. It offers a range of color alternatives to those such as the Birman or Persian, both of which are also renowned for their gentle dispositions.

RAGDOLL, SEAL MITTED POINT
Female

RAGDOLL, BLUE MITTED POINT
Male

RUSSIAN BLUE

HISTORY: The history of the Russian Blue is not known for sure. However, it is generally held that the breed is of Russian origin. Certainly, the first cats of this type came from that country and were known as Archangel cats for many years. They were first exhibited in England during 1880 and thereafter were largely developed by the British, as well as by breeders in Sweden. It is from England that the first examples were exported to the USA about 1900, or maybe even some years earlier.

To what degree the original Russian type exists today is a moot point, because both the Siamese and the British Blue were used to revitalize the breed following World War II. During the 1950s and 1960s breeders made efforts to move away from the strong influence of foreign type, so today's breed reflects this, probably more so in the USA than elsewhere. Apart from the color, the other important characteristic of the breed is the quality of its beautiful double coat. Its popularity on both sides of the Atlantic is about the same.

ALLOWABLE OUTCROSSES: None.

RECOGNITION: All associations.

DESCRIPTION

Head: A short wedge (GCCF) or a medium wedge (CFA). In profile the nose and forehead are straight and meet at a slight angle level with the upper edge of the eye. There is no stop. The whisker pads are prominent. The neck is long and slender.

Ears: Large, wide at their base and tapering to a narrow rounded tip. They are set vertical to the head (GCCF) or as much on the side as on the top of the head (CFA). The hair on the ears is short, giving the ear an almost translucent appearance.

RUSSIAN BLUE
Male, Quadruple Grand Champion

Eyes: Set wide apart and almond-shaped (GCCF), aperture rounded (CFA). The eye color is a vivid green, which may take time to be fully evident in kittens.

Body: Long and graceful. Medium strong bone. Never cobby nor svelte.

Legs & Feet: Long and slender with fine bones. The paws are small and oval.

Tail: Long and slender, tapering from base to tip, which should not be blunt nor whip-like.

Coat: Quite unique to the breed, the coat is plush, short and very dense. Its texture is smooth and silky. A good double coat is absolutely essential.

Color: A clear blue, even throughout its length, other than the tips of the guard hairs, which are silver. In the UK a medium blue is preferred, but in the USA the lighter shades are more favored. The coat must be free from tabby markings, shading, tipping and ticking in adult cats of the UK. However, some tipping must be present in order to create the desired silvery sheen. The CFA standard states that 'A definite contrast should be noted between the ground color and tipping.' In the UK, New Zealand and other countries, the Russian Blue is now seen in both black and blue varieties.

Remarks: The Russian Blue is a quiet cat as felines go and makes an obvious alternative to the Korat, Chartreuse, or British Blue, the only other long-established examples of the blue color in shorthaired cats. It is an elegant-looking breed well deserving of its popular status. In its long-haired form, the Russian Blue is known as the Nebelung and has gained group V recognition with TICA.

RUSSIAN BLUE
Female

RUSSIAN BLUE

RUSSIAN BLUE
Male

SCOTTISH FOLD

History: The mutation that is the basis of this breed was found in a farm cat in Perthshire, Scotland in 1961. Her name was Susie. She was a pure white shortcoated cat. From her offspring are descended all Scottish Folds. The breed arrived in the USA about 1970 and has proved very popular as it has in many other countries. However, it is not recognized in its homeland because of the potential side effects associated with the dominant gene mutation. If this condition is in the homozygous (double) state, the kittens may be unable to walk and may suffer various other abnormalities. When breeding Folds it is therefore necessary to mate a Fold cat with a normal-eared breed, the British or American Shorthair being the standard recommendation. Doing so thus will yield a 50% chance of producing Fold- and non-Fold-eared kittens.

ALLOWABLE OUTCROSSES: British or American Shorthairs.

RECOGNITION: All American associations.

DESCRIPTION

Head: Round and with full cheeks. The whisker pads are well developed and the head is carried on a short thick neck. The nose is short. While there is a nose break this should not be in any way well defined.

Ears: The feature of the breed, the ears are neatly folded forward. The smaller and tighter the fold the better, so they complement the rounded cranium effect. The tips are rounded.

Eyes: Large, well rounded and set far apart due to the broad nose. They exhibit just a slight slant towards the ears. The eyes, because of the reduced ear size, tend to be an essential part of the facial expression. Their appearance can be made the greater or the lesser based on the color of the surrounding fur.

SCOTTISH FOLD, BLUE MACKEREL TABBY
Male

SCOTTISH FOLD, DILUTE CALICO
Female, Grand Champion

SCOTTISH FOLD, CALICO AND WHITE
Female, Grand Champion

Body: Medium in size and of rounded appearance. The shoulder and rump should be of the same width. Overall, this is a cobby-type cat as would be expected from its British and American outcrossings.

Legs & Feet: Short and thick with round paws. The leg thickness is a side effect of the Fold mutation.

Tail: While a long tapering tail is the preferred state, it will often be found that the tail is thicker than in most breeds and may be shorter — again a side effect of the fold mutation.

Coat: Short, dense and resilient, the fur is hard and exhibits a high gloss as is seen in its outcross breeds.

Color: You can have a Scottish Fold in any color or pattern other than that of the pointed (Himalayan), chocolate and lilac. These, however, will appear in due course as they have in many other shorthaired breeds. Their eye color, paw pads and nose leather colors should be appropriate to the coat color.

Bad Faults: Kinked or foreshortened tail and a tail that lacks flexibility due to undue thickness. Incorrect eye color and ears that are semierect.

Remarks: The Scottish Fold is a very appealing breed with a quite unique facial expression. It is a pity there are associated problems that should give potential owners cause to discuss the breed with their veterinarian, especially if they plan to become breeders. A longhaired Fold is also available and this is equally attractive.

SCOTTISH FOLD, BROWN CLASSIC TABBY AND WHITE
Male   Grand Champion

LONGHAIRED SCOTTISH FOLD, BROWN
CLASSIC TABBY
Male, Kitten

SCOTTISH FOLD, BLUE MAKEREL TABBY
AND WHITE
Female, Kitten

SIAMESE

HISTORY: Along with the Persian, the Siamese has had a tremendous influence in the development of the cat fancy. Apart from being the second most popular breed for many years in most countries, it has been instrumental in passing its pattern and type to many other breeds. The Siamese appeared in the very first cat show that was held in London in 1871. Thereafter, there was a steady stream of imports. The breed reached the USA around the turn of the century. Just how old the breed is we will probably never know, but it has undoubtedly been evident in Thailand (formerly Siam) for a few centuries — along with the Korat and possibly the Burmese.

The breed has strong associations with both the royalty of Siam and the temples of the Buddhists, both of whom are known to have kept carefully bred lines of these cats. The original imports to England and the USA were not the very svelte examples of today but were rather stockier. They have been streamlined by breeders over the years. The first imports were

SIAMESE, LILAC POINT
Female, Grand Champion

SIAMESE, SEAL POINT
Male, Grand Champion

of the seal point variety. The other colors arrived over the years — some as natural mutations within the breed, but others after selected programs using other breeds, such as the Russian Blue. Once the colors had been introduced the type was refined to be that of the true Siamese. In Britain and most other countries and associations, all pointed patterns are accepted as being Siamese. However, in the CFA only the originally accepted four colors are classed as Siamese, all others being regarded as a separate breed: the Colorpoint Shorthair. The Siamese is the epitome of what is termed the foreign type in both appearance and character. It is a feline that is noted for the use of its vocal chords and for its almost dog-like traits. It is a breed that displays a greater-than-normal cu-

riosity about its surroundings and a penchant for mischief.

ALLOWABLE OUTCROSSES: None.

RECOGNITION: All associations.

DESCRIPTION

Head: If an imaginary line is drawn across from the tips of the ears and then down to the nose it would form a perfect triangle. There is no whisker break and the nose is long and straight, showing no stop at the forehead. The neck is long and elegant. There should be at least the width of an eye between the eyes. In profile the head is wedge shaped and the bite is level.

Ears: Large and wide at their base, they taper to a rounded point. Their outer edge should be angled such as to continue the facial lines of a triangle.

Eyes: Oriental (almond) in shape, they are slanted slightly towards the nose. There must be no evidence of a squint (cross-eyed). The eye color is a deep vivid blue, regardless of coat color and pattern.

Body: Medium in size, long and svelte. The hips should never be wider than the shoulders, the abdomen is tight and the overall appearance is of a slim, firmly muscled cat.

Legs & Feet: Long and slim, the hind legs are longer than the front. The paws are small and oval. The legs and feet should be proportionate to the body to form a graceful whole.

Tail: Long and tapering to a fine point. Must be free of kinks.

Coat: Very short and fine in texture, the coat should display a high gloss and lay close to the body.

SIAMESE, CHOCOLATE POINT
Female

SIAMESE, CHOCOLATE LYNX POINT
Female, Grand Champion

Color: The four 'classic' Siamese colors are described here. Others that are accepted by most associations are also presented.

Seal Point: Mask, ears, legs, feet and tail a clearly defined dense seal brown. The body cream, shading to a pale fawn on the back. Paw pads and nose leather the same color as the points.

Chocolate Point: The points to be a warm milk chocolate. The ears should not be darker than the other points. The body is ivory, with no shading (CFA), or if at all, to be the color of the points (GCCF). Paw pads and nose leather chocolate or cinnamon-pink.

SIAMESE, SEAL POINT
Male, Grand Champion

SIAMESE, SEAL LYNX POINT
Female

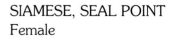

SIAMESE, SEAL POINT
Female

Blue Point: The points are a light blue (GCCF) or deep blue (CFA). The body is glacial white, shading gradually into blue on the back, the same cold tone as the points, but lighter. Paw pads and nose leather blue or slate colored.

Lilac (Frost) Point: The points are a pinkish or faded lilac color, described as a frosty gray with a pinkish tone in the USA. The body is off-white (magnolia) shading, if at all, to tone with the points (GCCF). The CFA states 'glacial white with no shading.' Paw pads and nose leather lavender pink to faded lilac.

The two other solid colors accepted by most associations are red point and cream point. To these can be added the tabby point, the tortie point, and the tortie tabby point. Each of these patterns is available in the major colors of the breed.

Bad Faults: A complete hood (no contrast in color on head), a kink in the tail, an eye squint, odd-sized eyes, incorrect eye color, lack of contrast between points and body colors, incorrect color on paw pads and nose leather, uneven bite.

SIAMESE, SEAL POINT
Female, Grand Champion

Remarks: The Siamese is the sort of breed people either love or dislike. Some find it altogether too skinny and vocal, others find these features the very essence of its appeal. There is no denying this is a breed that is quite unique and one that will always be both popular and a major player in the way that the cat fancy develops.

SIAMESE, CHOCOLATE LYNX POINT
Female, Kitten

SIAMESE, TORTIE POINT
Female, Kitten

SIAMESE, CHOCOLATE POINT
Female, Grand Champion

SIAMESE, RED POINT
Male

SIAMESE, SEAL LYNX POINT
Male, Kitten

SIAMESE, BLUE LYNX POINT
Male

SINGAPURA

HISTORY: Typical of many street cats found throughout Asia, the Singapura is unusual in that it is only the second natural breed to be recognized that sports a ticked coat — the other being the Abyssinian. The first imports into the USA commenced about 1975. The breed was initially dubbed the 'drain cat,' a title not likely to give it appeal. This has now been dropped, for it is a common name that could equally be applied to any feral street cats in Malaysia that have to fend for themselves. While the Singapura has gained recognition in all the American registries it remains a relatively rare breed.

ALLOWABLE OUTCROSSES: None.

RECOGNITION: All USA associations, but not in UK.

DESCRIPTION

Head: Rounded and with a definite whisker break. The nose is medium-short and the muzzle is broad. In profile the head is rounded and there is a slight stop below eye level.

Ears: Large, open at their base and tapering to a rounded tip.

Eyes: Large and almond-shaped, they are set at a slight angle. There should be at least the width of an eye between the eyes. Their color is gold, hazel or green, no other color being permitted.

Body: On the small side, muscular and somewhat stocky. The ideal is that the body and legs should be such that they form a square, not a rectangle as in most breeds.

Legs & Feet: Heavy boned, well muscled and tapering from the body to small oval feet.

Tail: Shorter than the body length and tapering to a blunted tip.

Coat: Very short, fine and laying close to the

SINGAPURA, SEPIA AGOUTI TABBY

body. Must display a satin-like sheen. The coat is longer in juveniles.

Color: Brown ticked. This is dark brown ticking on an old ivory ground. Muzzle, chin, chest and stomach to be the color of unbleached muslin. Paw pads rosy brown. Nose leather salmon with an outline in brown. The tail tip is brown. Some tabby markings may be evident on front and rear legs as well as on the forehead.

Bad Faults: Small ears and eyes, incorrect eye color, white lockets or buttons, barring on tail, whip-like tail, unbroken bracelets on legs.

Remarks: The Singapura is a pleasing feline of small size. Its appeal will probably always be limited because there are so many more strikingly marked and colored felines from which to choose.

SINGAPURA, SEPIA AGOUTI TABBY
Male

SNOWSHOE

HISTORY: One of the more recent breeds, the Snowshoe is still a developing feline variety. Essentially, it is a pointed breed with white feet. It is the result of crossing Siamese with bicolored American Shorthairs. The result is a very appealing cat. Breeding well-marked Snowshoes will not be easy due to the variability — and unpredictability — of the feet markings.

RECOGNITION: TICA; CFF.

DESCRIPTION

Head: The shape of the head is somewhat variable, depending upon the state of development of the particular line. The desired head is a modified wedge, neither too foreign nor rounded. The nose is straight and in profile there is no stop.

Ears: Large, open at their base and tapering to a rounded tip.

Eyes: Almond-shaped, they are large and display a slight slant towards the nose. Their color is a vivid blue. No other color is permitted.

Body: Medium in size, the body is lithe and muscular, being neither of the cobby shorthair type, nor the very svelte type of the Siamese.

Legs & Feet: Medium to long and slim. The paws are oval.

Tail: Of medium length and tapering gently to the tip.

Coat: Short, glossy and slightly coarse in texture, it lays close to the body.

Color: Presently there are just two accepted colors.

Seal Point: The mask is seal brown but broken by an inverted white 'V'. The extent of this white marking is in fact extremely variable in the breed, so the ideal is not often seen. The ears, legs and tail are also seal brown. The body is fawn paling on the undersides. The bib is white. Any shading should be of the points color. The white on the feet should ideally match; that is, the front feet should be evenly matched, as should the hind. The white on the hind legs goes higher up the leg than that on the front legs.

SNOWSHOE, BLUE PARTICOLOR POINT
Female

Blue Point: The mask, ears, tail and legs are a gray-blue. The body is a bluish white, which is paler on the undersides and invariably white on the throat and chest. The feet are white. The paw pads and nose leathers in either of the two colors will match the point's color or will be the color and/or pink.

Bad Faults: Incorrect eye color, kink in the tail, missing white on any foot, white lockets or buttons, body too cobby or too svelte, overlong fur.

Remarks: The Snowshoe will certainly be a breed that will gain wider recognition in the coming years. It combines the merits of a Siamese with those of an American Shorthair and includes the feet markings of a Birman to complete the package. There is no doubt that other colors will become available in due course.

SNOWSHOE, SEAL PARTICOLOR POINT
Male

SOMALI

HISTORY: The true origin of the Somali is a matter of conjecture within the cat fancy. Some say it is the result of crossing the Abyssinian with a Persian or other longhair and then, having introduced the recessive longhair gene, breeding out the type of the outcross. Others, in fact most in feline circles, accept that it was a spontaneous mutation that appeared in a litter of Abyssinians during the 1960s. Such longhaired Abys started to appear in the USA and Europe during the 1970s. The variety was given breed status during that decade.

In all aspects of its conformation the Somali is an Abyssinian, its differing look being the result of its longer fur. However, the standards for the two breeds do differ somewhat in the descriptions used.

ALLOWABLE OUTCROSSES: Abyssinian.

RECOGNITION: All associations.

DESCRIPTION

Head: A modified, slightly rounded wedge. The brow, cheek and profile lines all display gently rounded contours. There is a slight rise from the bridge of the nose to the forehead. In profile there is a slight nose break but not a whisker break, nor any tendency to a pointed 'fox-like' muzzle.

Ears: Large and set wide apart, they taper to a pointed tip. Ear tufts are desirable.

Eyes: Large, almond-shaped and set well apart. The eyes are highlighted by a dark lid skin encircled by a lighter colored area. Pencil lines extend from the eye to the ear. The color of the eyes is amber, hazel or green, the richer and deeper the better.

Body: Medium long, lithe and graceful. The back is just slightly arched. The body represents a balance between the cobby and svelte types.

Legs & Feet: Medium in size and well

SOMALI, RUDDY
Female, Kitten

SOMALI, FAWN
Male, Champion

SOMALI, FAWN
Male, Champion

muscled. The paws are oval in shape and tufted with hair.

Tail: Longish due to the generous fur that is similar to the brush of a fox in its density.

Coat: Very soft, extremely fine and dense. A good double coat should be evident and display at least three bands of ticking. The length is medium except on the shoulder where a shorter fur is permitted. Preference is given to cats that exhibit a good ruff and breeches so a full coated appearance is imparted.

Color: The range of colors accepted in the UK is more extensive than that of the USA. The original colors were ruddy (usual) and red (sorrel) but today you can have the Somali in the following shades: chocolate, blue, lilac, fawn, ruddy silver, red silver, chocolate silver, blue silver, lilac silver, fawn silver. You are referred to the Abyssinian for more detail on these colors, together with the appropriate paw pad and nose leather colors. It should be born in mind that the ticked effect is not as apparent in this breed as in the Abyssinian, due to the longer fur, which tends to break up the pattern.

Bad Faults: Cobby or Siamese type, white anywhere on the body other than in the area of the chin, lips and nostrils, unbroken necklaces, leg bars, and tabby stripes on the body or tail. Kink in tail.

Remarks: The Somali is a most attractive breed offering long yet very manageable fur. In its ruddy (usual) coloring it has the appearance of a wild feline yet is as gentle as any other breed. Its popularity is steadily, and justifiably, rising all over the world.

SOMALI, SORREL "RED"
Female, Grand Champion

SPHYNX

HISTORY: Hairless (or nearly so) cats, dogs, and other mammals have occurred many times over the years. Generally, they are wisely regarded as freaks and, if kept, never bred from. However, when a hairless kitten was found in a normal litter born in Ontario, Canada in 1966, it was retained to became the basis of a new breed - the Sphynx. Although it initially gained some acceptance with certain registries, one or two of these later revoked its status.

ALLOWABLE OUTCROSSES: American Shorthair; Devon Rex (TICA).

RECOGNITION: TICA.

DESCRIPTION

The Sphynx has the appearance of a foreign-type cat with very large ears and a modified wedge face. The eyes are almond to round in shape and exhibit a slight oriental slant. The body is long and muscular. The chest is broad and round. The legs are long and slim, often bowed due to the broad chest. The paws are small and oval. The tail is long and displays a slight taper to its tip. The coat is, of course, virtually absent, being represented by a few down hairs scattered over the body, generally in the area of the ears, tail tip and feet. The skin is variable in the extent of its wrinkles, which are most obvious on the legs, face, neck and shoulders. The breed is seen in all recognized colors and patterns, these being seen in the skin coloration.

Unless the unusual appeals to you, it is most unlikely the Sphynx will be on your list of favorite breeds. Clearly, it will suffer in all weather conditions. It is a breed that cannot have any realistic future in the cat fancy other than as a breed people look at from a purely curios viewpoint. In terms of its nature, it is like any other feline: quite adorable.

SPHYNX
Male, Champion

SPHYNX, BLUE CLASSIC TORBIE
Female, Kitten

SPHYNX, BROWN CLASSIC TABBY AND
WHITE
Male

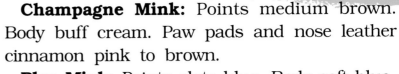
Champagne Mink: Points medium brown. Body buff cream. Paw pads and nose leather cinnamon pink to brown.

Blue Mink: Points slate blue. Body soft blue-gray shading to lighter tone on underparts. Paw pads and nose leather blue-gray.

Honey Mink: Points pewter gray. Body golden cream, preferably with an apricot cast. Paw pads and nose leather a caramel pink.

Platinum Mink: Pewter gray, but may exhibit a lavender cast. Body pale silvery gray with warm overtones. Not white or cream. Paw pads and nose leather lavender gray-pink.

In all colors there should be a clear distinction between the color of the points and that of the body. However, in the red or cream points this will be less evident than in the darker colors. The mask and ears are connected by faint tabby tracings. Tabby bracelets are seen in the reds of the British Tonkinese.

Bad Faults: Kink in tail, cobby or svelte types, incorrect eye color, white lockets or buttons, definite nose break (stop).

TONKINESE, CHAMPAGNE MINK
Female

TONKINESE, NATURAL MINK
Male

Remarks: The Tonkinese is a handsome breed that will have appeal to those who like the Siamese character, but prefer a little more meat on their cats and a somewhat less extreme type. When breeding these cats there will be a need to make careful selection from the kittens in order to stabilize the type required by the standard of your country.

TONKINESE, PLATINUM MINK
Male

The Tonkinese is similar to the Siamese in color but is a more solidly built cat. Photo by Isabelle Francais

TURKISH ANGORA

HISTORY: The Angora is named for Ankara, the capital of Turkey. The breed is very old and may well be the oldest of the longhaired breeds, along with the Persian. Both have been known to exist for many centuries. When they first started to appear in England and France during the 19th century, the differences between the two were not as striking as they are today. As a result, indiscriminate crossbreeding took place. Steadily, the more woolly and profusely coated Persians became the more fashionable. The Angora, as a breed, virtually disappeared — the same happening in the USA.

Ankara zoo maintains a breeding population of pure white Angoras. In the 1960s pairs of these were exported to the USA, where the breed re-established itself and gained recognition with all of the registries. In the UK some imports from Turkey were made. However, hybridizing with Siamese also took place in order to 'manufacture' an original-looking Angora.

ALLOWABLE OUTCROSSES: None.

RECOGNITION: All associations.

An Amber-eyed white female Turkish Angora. Photo by Larry Levy.

DESCRIPTION

Head: Small to medium, it is a longish wedge that commences at the nose and flares out in straight lines to the ears, forming a triangle when viewed from the front. There is no whisker break. The nose is medium-long and straight, with no stop at the forehead. In profile the muzzle forms a fine wedge. The head is carried on a long slender neck.

Ears: Set high on the head, they appear quite large. Wide at their base, they taper to a pointed tip. They may be tufted.

Eyes: Large and almond-shaped, they display a slight slant towards the ears.

Body: Of medium size, long, graceful and tubular. The hips and shoulders are the same width, the abdomen is tight.

Legs & Feet: Long and slim, the hind legs are longer than the front. Well muscled and furred, the legs look more substantial than the reality of the underlying bone. The paws are small and round, with hair tufts between the toes.

Tail: Long, thin and tapering (GCCF) or long and tapering, wide at base, narrow at end (CFA).

Coat: Very fine and silky, displaying a beautiful sheen. There is no (more correctly, *minimal*) woolly undercoat. The hair on the ruff and undersides is longer than that of the spine and may exhibit a wavy tendency. The tail hair is long and plume-like.

TURKISH ANGORA, BLUE
Female, Triple Grand Champion

extend below the level of the eyes, nor beyond the base of the back of the ears. There should be a blaze of white separating the markings on the head. The tail is auburn and may be faintly ringed; the color may extend just a little way onto the rump. Small patches of color on the body are undesirable but should not disqualify an otherwise good specimen. The paw pads and nose leather are pink.

Cream: The color is a much more pale shade than the auburn. Its placement is as for the auburn.

Bad Faults: Siamese, Persian, British or American Shorthair type. Kink in tail, squinted (cross) eyes, undershot, overshot or misaligned jaw. Incorrect eye color, or excessive color marks on the body.

Remarks: The Turkish Van is much more popular in the UK than is the Angora and is gaining devotees with each passing year in the USA and elsewhere. Its coat and markings are quite distinctive. While the coat is long it is also very manageable if groomed on a regular basis. It is a breed that is sure to gain its rightful place as a very popular long-hair. It may be assumed that more colors will be added in the coming years.

TURKISH VAN, RED AND WHITE
Male, Kitten

TURKISH VAN, RED AND WHITE
Female, Kitten

The
Allure
of the
Cat